LEARN GUITAR: INTERMEDIATE COURSE

BY

JUSTIN MOSS

COPYRIGHT

COPYRIGHT © TEXT AND IMAGES, JUSTIN MOSS, 2015

ALL RIGHTS RESERVED

THE MORAL RIGHT OF THE AUTHOR HAS BEEN ASSERTED

ISBN 978-0-9941277-1-6

ALL RIGHTS RESERVED. NO PART OF THIS PUBLICATION MAY BE REPRODUCED, STORED IN A RETRIEVAL SYSTEM OR TRANSMITTED IN ANY FORM BY ANY MEANS ELECTRONIC, MECHANICAL, PHOTOCOPYING, RECORDING OR OTHERWISE, WITHOUT PRIOR PERMISSION FROM THE COPYRIGHT OWNER.

PUBLISHED BY JMLM PUBLICATIONS, 2015

WEBSITE: http://learnguitar.nz

EMAIL: justin@learnguitar.nz

FEEDBACK

"If you are thinking about it buy it now with confidence."
bookdude

"Am on my 4th lesson now and loving it!"
tashlynian

"I love the dvd's it's easy to learn from and understand."
katcat2

"It's just like having a tutor beside you."
rollyn2

"Learned more in 2 weeks from the book and DVD than in the last 5 years."
bristolsteve

"Well presented, easy to follow and gets straight into it, no messing about."
elbino

"Top Rate Tuition for a fraction of the price."
johnjohn8

"Very impressed at the professional presentation and layout."
rayurlich

"Very clear and easy to follow!"
agy321

ABOUT

Justin Moss has been playing the guitar since he was sixteen-years-old, and started teaching full-time not long after that. Many years on Justin is as passionate about the guitar as today as he was when he first picked it up.

"The guitar is a fantastic instrument," he says, "it encompasses every style of music, can generate any emotion, and is as pleasurable to play as it is to listen to."

With his unique and effective method for learning to play guitar, he has had many successes with private guitar students, and taught thousands more around the world with his series of Learn Guitar Courses.

CONTENTS

COPYRIGHT	2
FEEDBACK	3
ABOUT	4
Session 1	7
Lesson 1 - The Chromatic Scale	8
Lesson 2 - C-Major Scale Pattern 1	10
Lesson 3 - Power Chords	15
Lesson 4 - Pentatonic Scales	17
Lesson 5 - Lead techniques	20
Lesson 6 - Power Chord Blues	23
Session 2	25
Lesson 1 – Chord Construction	26
Lesson 2 – Let's start constructing some chords	28
Lesson 3 – Minor Chords	32
Lesson 4 – Sevenths & Major-Sevenths	34
Lesson 5 – Minor-Sevenths	36
Lesson 6 - Using our Chord Construction for Songs	37
Lesson 7 – Natural Minor Scales	42
Lesson 8 – Song Construction	46
Session 3	53
Lesson 1 – Scales	54
Lesson 2 – A Return to the Blues	56
Lesson 3 – Fingerpicking	61
Lesson 4 – Arpeggio Work	63
Lesson 5 – More work for the left hand.	66
Session 4	73
Lesson 1 – C-Major Scale Pattern 3	74
Lesson 2 – Developing the Blues Shuffle Rhythm Further.	76
Lesson 3 – Fingerpicking	82
Lesson 4 – Arpeggio's	85
Session 5	87
Lesson 1 – Scale Work	88

Lesson 2 – How about some Jazz?	89
Lesson 3 – True Blues in E	94
Session 6	**101**
Lesson 1 – C-Major Scale Pattern 5	102
Lesson 2 – Songwriting	103
Lesson 3 – The Circle of Fifths	107
Lesson 4 – Blues for Sam (12 Bar Blues)	110
Session 7	**115**
Lesson 1 - A Quick Foray	116
Lesson 2 - Hou Day X 7	119
Session 8	**122**
Lesson 1 - Truest Kind	123
Lesson 2 - The Old Ballad Song	129
HAVE YOU CONSIDERED...	**135**

SESSION 1

Hello! And congratulations! If you're starting this course, then you have most likely finished a beginner course (and passed!). By this, it means that you are able to play the guitar quite competently and are looking to further your skills even more.

That is what the course is about! With these lessons, we embark on a far more advanced nature of learning than the beginners' courses. The lessons here are difficult and will require a lot of exercise and constant practice. Most of these exercises are mind-numbingly boring, and most have to be done every day, again and again. But, if you do them, and if you do them properly, the benefits will be amazing.

You'll be a far better player in a far shorter time than you could possibly imagine. But you've got to do the practice. Do the time. Reap the reward.

Read on. Practice. Enjoy.

Good luck and good playing.

LESSON 1 - THE CHROMATIC SCALE

You should all be very familiar with the initial chromatic scale that we learned in the beginner's course. This is merely an extension of that scale, and on paper doesn't look a lot harder that the old one.

In truth though, this is far, far more difficult than the earlier chromatic scale.

It is (and was with the old one as well!) a technique builder. Pure and simple. Hard on the hands, difficult for the fingers, but important that we get it right.

As you can see, it runs across two stings, being the 2nd and 1st. You start with the open 2nd string note (B) and then ascend to the note on the fourth fret, which you play with your little finger i.e. stay with our technique of 1 finger per fret and staying in position. That's the easy part.

Now, while holding ALL you fingers still against the notes on the 2nd string, pluck the open 1st string note (E). Then, while holding your fingers down on the second, third and fourth frets of the 2nd string, place your 1st finger on the first fret 1st string. Do the same with your second finger against the second fret 1st string (while still holding your 1st, 3rd and 4th fingers in place). Then do the third finger note. And the fourth finger note on the 1st string.

You should now have ascended to the highest note of our scale. All your fingers should still be against the fretboard.

Now descend back to the open 1st string note. Place ALL four fingers as one against the four notes on the 2nd string and descend down through that string as well until you reach the open 2nd string note.

That is the complete chromatic scale. Now you've got to do it again. 20 times a day, actually.

The most important part about doing this scale is your discipline. The scale must be played evenly and slowly. Speed is of no consequence and will most likely make the scale sound stunted. If it is not played smooth and consistent, it's not worth playing in the first place.

The second most important part is your left-hand discipline. Making those fingers do as you wish, with some clamped on the second string and some on the first is no easy task. It will take practice and more practice to get it right, but I think that you knew that already.

Of a further note, there is no reason that you cannot use a down/up picking motion with the right hand. Up till now we've kept things mostly simple and used downstrokes, but it's time to start alternating down/up etc. Keep an eye that it is consistent also, being down up down up down up etc and not down up down down up up.

Here's the diagram.

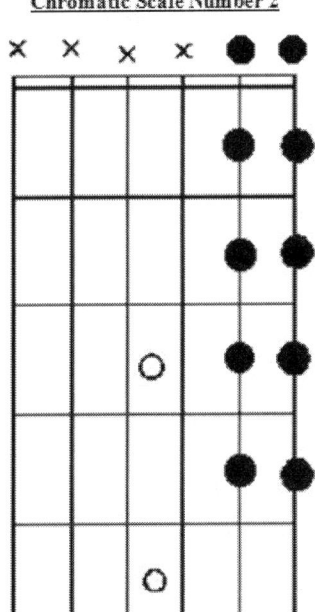

VIDEO ACCOMPANIMENT IS AVAILABLE FOR THIS LESSON

Head to http://learnguitar.nz

LESSON 2 - C-MAJOR SCALE PATTERN 1

Now, we all know how to create a major scale on paper don't we.

We use our formula:

W W H W W W H

Put that between our notes and we have a major scale.

Now we also know that W stands for Whole Step, and that H stands for Half Step

Now on our guitar, a Whole Step is equal to two frets, a Half Step one fret.

So with all this knowledge, we should have no trouble putting working out the notes for a C-Major scale and putting them onto our guitar.

I'm sure you all know the notes of the C-Major by heart, so here's the scale.

C D E F G A B C

To put it on the guitar is quite simple.

We'll start with what we know. The open notes of the six strings.

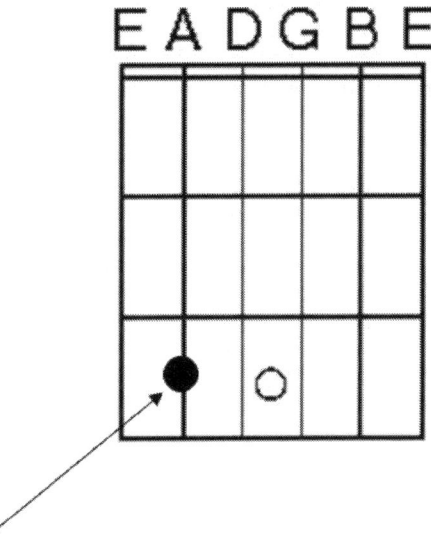

Lets find our C-Note (Root Note) for the scale. Know how we found it?

We'll there's a WHOLE STEP gap between A (the open 5th string note) and B, so that means that B is on the second fret (a WHOLE STEP is equal to 2 FRETS), and there is HALF STEP gap between B and C (a HALF STEP is equal to 1 FRET). That means that we have a C note on the third fret, 5th string, as the arrow points to.

Do you understand how we arrived at the C note? If not go through it again.

C — W — D — W — E — H — F — W — G — W — A — W — B — H — C

Okay, so we have a root note.

C (Third fret, 5th string)

Let's look at our scale again.

Okay, from our C note, let's move on.

We know there is a WHOLE STEP between C and D, so the next logical place to play D is going to be the Open 4th string note.

11

There is a WHOLE STEP between D and E as well, so the E note is going to be on the second fret 4th string.

We have a HALF STEP between E and F, so the F note is going to be on the third fret 4th string.

And our scale is starting to take shape.

Here's a diagram of the notes we've added so far.

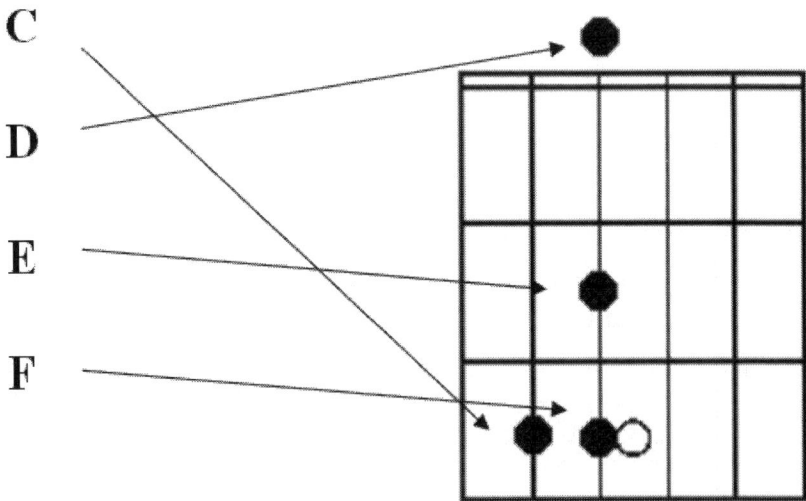

So, from there, shouldn't be too difficult to follow through the rest of the scale. You'll reach the next C note on the 2nd string first fret, and after that, just keep going until we reach the G note on the 1st string, third fret. We'll stop there because any more notes will pull our left-hand out of position, which we do not want to do.

If you're feeling really tricky, then do then notes down to the open E on the 6th string. They are part of our scale also. When you think you've got it right, turn the page and check your scale against ours.

C-Major Scale – Pattern 1

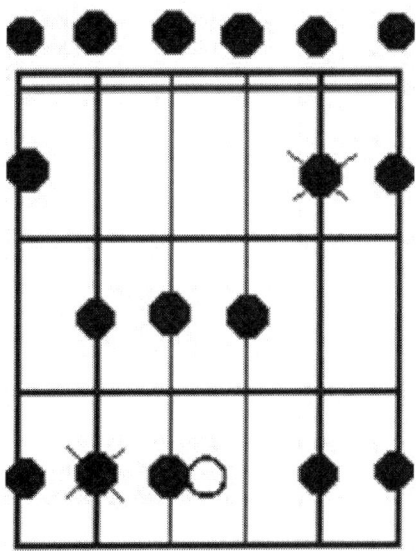

Here it is in TAB

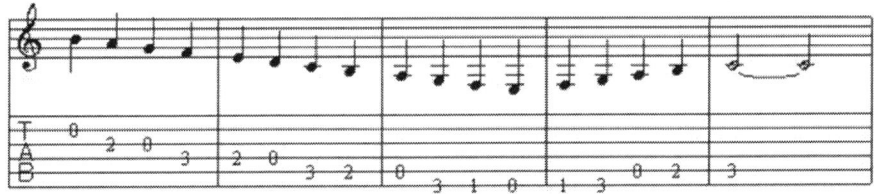

Don't ever Forget the Rules of Playing Scales

With any scale, the most important factors are playing the notes EVENLY, SMOOTHLY, CONSISTENTLY, and also ensuring the COORDINATION between your hands is right.

EVENLY: It is sometimes easy to play the easy part of the scale quickly and slow the hard parts down. This is wrong. A scale should always be played EVENLY, with all parts played at the same speed. A scale not played this way will earn you a rap over the knuckles by your teacher.

SMOOTHLY: Very closely related to EVENLY, SMOOTHLY is about playing each note with matching values. Your fingers on the left hand should take on an almost mechanical feel, fingers going up and down like pistons in a smooth fashion.

CONSISTENTLY: It's no great sigh of relief to pull off the chromatic scale in front front of your teacher. The only thing that will stop you playing a scale the same every time is if you are either, playing it too fast, or not playing it enough. Practice it at the same speed with no aspirations to make it any faster, and do that every time, and that it CONSISTENCY.

COORDINATION: This is the trickiest of all. Your right hand should pluck the Note at the exact same time the left hand finger pushes down on the string. It's harder than you might think, and you really have to listen for it. There should be no gap between notes played one after another; your scale should show great COORDINATION between left and right hands. If it does, then you're most of the way there to playing EVENLY, SMOOTHLY, and CONSISTENTLY.

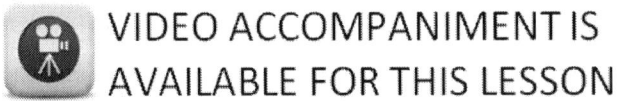
VIDEO ACCOMPANIMENT IS AVAILABLE FOR THIS LESSON

Head to http://learnguitar.nz

LESSON 3 - POWER CHORDS

Power chords are chords that are predominantly used in Rock, Blues and Heavy Metal music. They have their place in other forms of music both on the electric and acoustic guitar as well.

They are simple, effective, not hard to play and have a easy sort of a sound and feel about them. They are also known as 5ths and you may quite often see a power chord written as A5 for example, or G5 etc.

To play one, all we need to do is take a standard BARRE chord, and play only the two lowest strings (lowest as in pitch, not height on the guitar!)

For example, look at the chords below. You see the E-Shape Barre Chord, and then you see the Power Chord to match. Notice that it uses the ROOT note of the chord and then the next string down only.

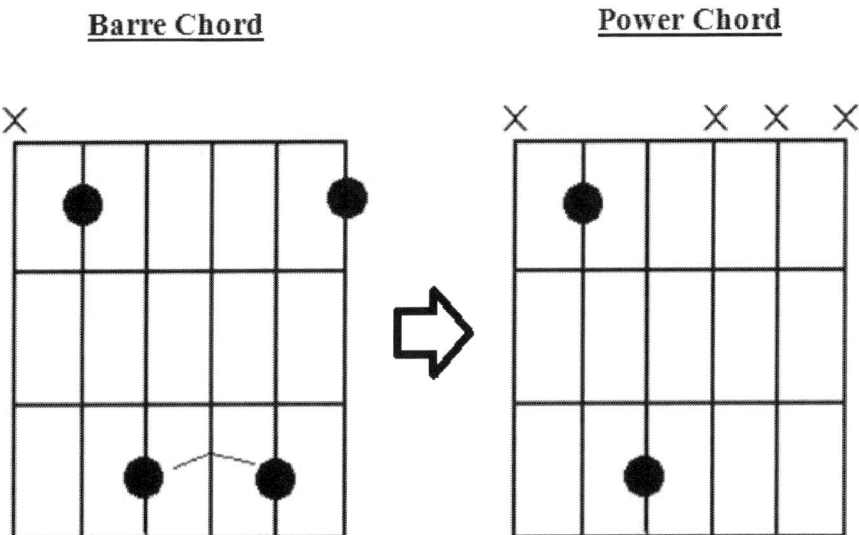

See how they work? Pretty easy, isn't it?

Power chords are unique in that they can be substituted over almost ANY chord!

This is what gives them their flexibility and is why they are so widely used.

Power chords don't differentiate between MAJOR and MINOR. You can use a power chord as a substitute for a MINOR chord as easily as MAJOR.

For some exercise, try playing some of our chord progressions using only Power Chords. Try playing 12-Bar Blues with only Power Chords.

They sound great, and as the name suggests, do have a certain power about them that can give a song a little extra kick or boost at certain points.

Head to http://learnguitar.nz

LESSON 4 - PENTATONIC SCALES

In the beginner's course, you may remember learning the Em Pentatonic Scale.

Well, all we're going to do it again in this lesson, and then a little more. First, a little background.

Pentatonic Scales are modern scales that are used heavily in all styles of music. They have only five notes (hence penta) and with that, there are fewer notes to play with, which can reduce their flexibility, but more importantly, reduce significantly the number of bad notes you can hit. Their use is without a doubt more widespread than any other type of scale in the entire music spectrum. Their importance therefore, is very high, and so they are the first type of scale that we will actively begin to use in our songs, our lead and our fills.

The way we learn our pentatonic scale is somewhat different to the major scale for the time being. With the major scale, we've done all the theory and we know how to work out the scale for ourselves. With the pentatonic, it's just a shape like a chord – here it is, accept it!

Below is the Minor Pentatonic shape, and alongside the Em Pentatonic scale that we learned earlier.

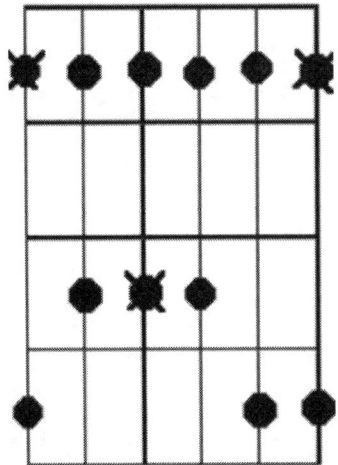 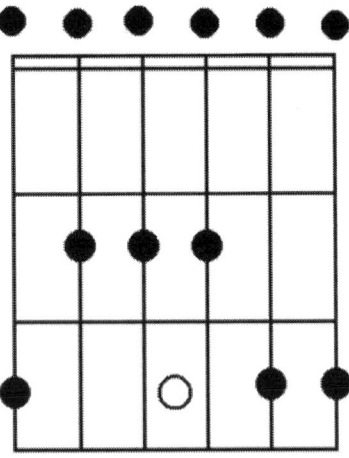

Right then, so an Am Pentatonic Scale would be the standard Minor Pentatonic Scale on the 5th fret.

To practice the pentatonic scale, is important that you use CONSISTENT up/down strokes with the pick.

When starting with the lowest root note, begin with an up stroke, and keep it all down/up/down/up etc etc from there.

We will NOT be playing this scale at all using all down or all up!

Some Practice with Minor Pentatonic Scales.

- Try practicing them in all the different positions up and down the fretboard. We haven't really done a lot except barre chords on the higher frets and this will be a good chance to start familiarising ourselves with them.
- Take the Minor Pentatonic Scale and play it with the root note on the 12th fret. What scale do we have? An Em pentatonic. It's exactly the same scale as our other Em Pentatonic Scale, just an octave higher.
- We will begin learning some lead and riff techniques shortly with the Minor Pentatonic Scales soon, so learn them well and by heart.

VIDEO ACCOMPANIMENT IS AVAILABLE FOR THIS LESSON

Head to http://learnguitar.nz

LESSON 5 - LEAD TECHNIQUES

Hammer on's and Pull Off's

The most basic and most important techniques of lead guitar are the Hammer on's and the Pull Off's. They're simple to play once you get the hang of it and have a sound to them which is unbeatable.

We'll start with the Hammer On.

Okay the theory is simple.

Pluck an open string, let's say the first string. Let it ring for a second, then plop your third finger of the left hand onto the third fret 1st string. The string should still be ringing, only the note will have changed to the fretted note on the third fret

Get it?

Try again. And again and again until you can get it quite smooth.

Now try it with your second finger onto the second fret. Then the first finger onto the first fret. How about the fourth finger onto the fourth fret? Now that one is a bit trickier!

For the time being, concentrate on the first, second and third fingers hammering onto the first, second and third frets. Practice getting the hammer smooth and fluid, just like our scales with no gap or buzz between the notes.

When you think that you have the first string going great, move onto the same exercise on the 2nd, 3rd, 4th, 5th and 6th strings.

How Hammer On's look in music and TAB.

With our music, the two (or more) notes they represent are joined by a curved line. This is called Legato in theory, which is Italian for smooth or flowing.

See the examples below.

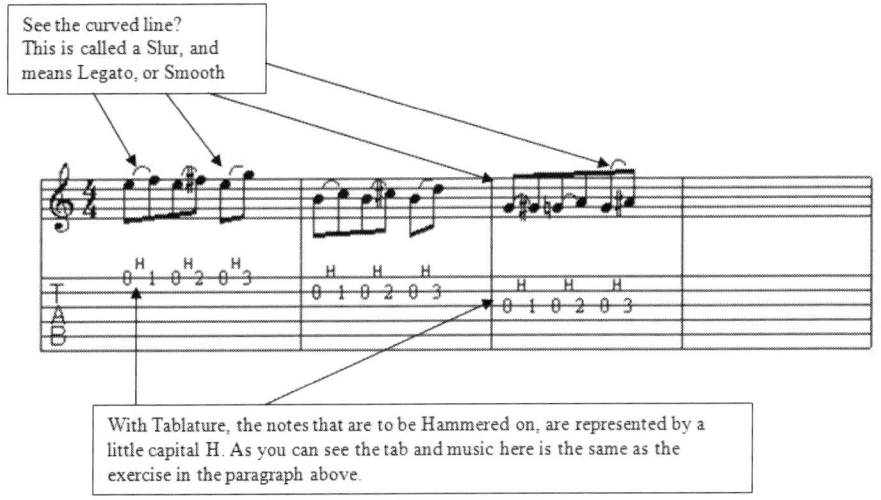

The Hammer On exercises should be played at least 20 times every day.

Pull Off's

The other predominant lead technique is the Pull Off. They are quite literally the opposite of the hammer on, and instead of banging your finger down, you get a good grip with the tip, and then pull it off, leaving the string still ringing.

They are also Legato, and are to be played smoothly, with no muting or buzz again.

Let's practice.

Okay, finger the third fret, 1st string note with your third finger. Now pluck the string, let it ring a moment, then pull your finger off, leaving the open string still ringing true.

Try again.

Now do it on the second fret with your second finger. First with first.

Make sure you get it smooth, and practice until you can get the open string to ring through as loud and as clear as if you'd actually picked it.

When you think you've got it going quite well, try the 2nd string, then the 3rd, 4th 5th and 6th.

How Pull Off's look in music and TAB.

Again, like the Hammer On's, Pull Off's are shown on the Music script joined with a curved line. There is no difference on the script between how a pull off and a hammer on looks, and it's only on the tab that there is any difference, being that instead of a little H for hammer on, there is a little P for Pull Off.

Pretty simple really.

Have a look at the examples below.

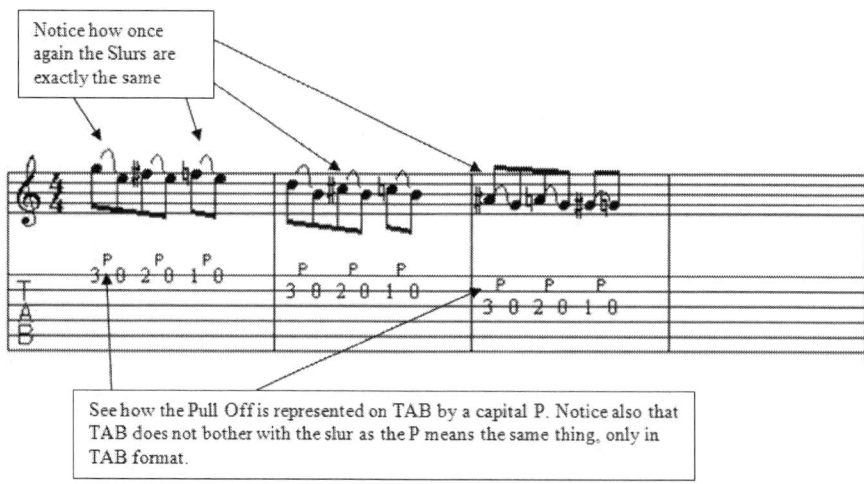

The Pull Off exercises should be played at least 20 times every day.

Head to http://learnguitar.nz

LESSON 6 - POWER CHORD BLUES

Here is a piece to test what we've learned to date.

Power Chord Blues

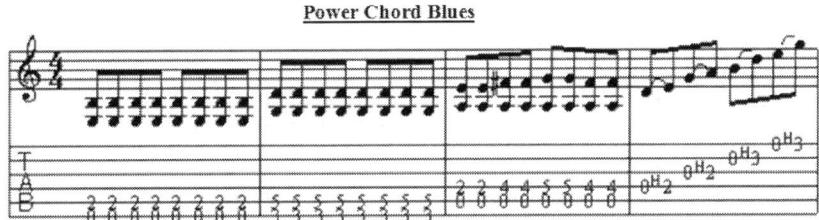

Make sure that you use the correct fingers as shown.

For the licks at the end of each line, these are being played in the Em Pentatonic scale, so use fingering the same as the scale. Try to get it playing well and consistent.

Well, that's the first session of the Fingers of Fire Guitar School Intermediate Course.

At this stage you will have noticed that it is all exercises and techniques.

There is quite a jump from what you've learned previously to what we're learning now. The techniques are a departure from the standard chords and right hand techniques that were so pushed previously.

Also, you will have noticed a lack of songs or examples to play to. This session is purely about exercise and discipline! Every one of the scales and techniques must be practiced every day. Proficiency is not hard to gain, but it does take a commitment from the player.

Why is it like this, you might ask?

Well, we're going to do the hard work now, and then we'll reap the rewards later.

Coming up, we've got theory, more scales, more exercises, more techniques and more hard work. But after that, we've got some of the best sounding songs and the greatest sounding pieces for solo guitar and guitar with accompaniment that you'll hear – and you'll be able to really enjoy them if you put the labour in now!

So play hard, practice hard, and make sure that your practice schedule contains all the exercises in here.

Next week, we'll learn a song, and we'll learn how it works and why.

Good luck and good playing.

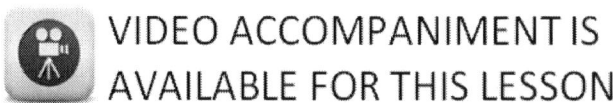

VIDEO ACCOMPANIMENT IS AVAILABLE FOR THIS LESSON

Head to http://learnguitar.nz

SESSION 2

LESSON 1 – CHORD CONSTRUCTION

Okay, to start with in this Session, we're going to do some work on our theory – an exciting part of theory and the guitar – Chord Construction.

To date we've been merrily playing away with our chords, changing the bass note, adding our little finger where we can to enhance the pieces, and generally picking, fingerpicking or strumming our way into musical happiness. Well, we're going to explore where the chords come from and why.

To start with, we'd better have a look at the notes on the first five frets of our guitar. You should make an effort to learn these by heart. It's not hard, as all the notes follow the standard Whole-Step, Half-Step intervals between the notes. For example, even without the diagram, we all know that the open note of the 2nd string is B. We also know that there is a Half-Step interval between B and C, so logically the note of C can be found on the 1st fret of the 2nd string.

Following that same logic, there is a Whole-Step interval between C and D – so D must fall on the 3rd fret 2nd string etc etc. Easy really, isn't it.

Anyway, the diagram below has all the notes for our first five frets, which we'll need for our chord construction.

Study it hard and learn them as well as you can.

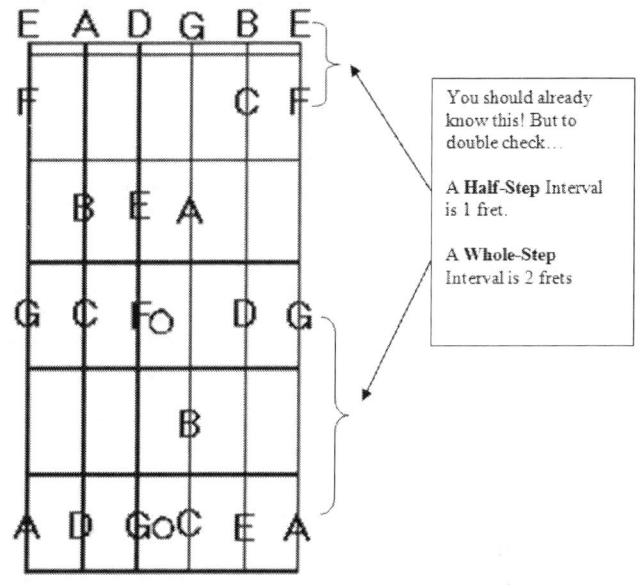

Take note to ensure that you correctly know the intervals between the notes.
i.e. that there is a Half-Step Interval between B & C as well as E & F

You should already know this! But to double check...

A **Half-Step** Interval is 1 fret.

A **Whole-Step** Interval is 2 frets

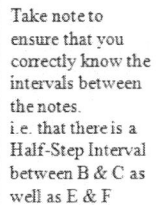 **VIDEO ACCOMPANIMENT IS AVAILABLE FOR THIS LESSON**

Head to http://learnguitar.nz

LESSON 2 – LET'S START CONSTRUCTING SOME CHORDS

First thing we need is our Major Scale. We'll use C-Major to keep things simple for the time being.

Here's the notes.

C D E F G A B C

Now, each note is given a number as well, starting at 1 and going through to 8, which isn't called 8 but Octave instead.

C	D	E	F	G	A	B	C
1	**2**	**3**	**4**	**5**	**6**	**7**	**Oct**

In this way, the notes of C-Major are referred to by their number as well. For example, G is known as the 5th of C-Major, A is the 6th, E the 3rd etc etc

Get the idea?

Good.

Now to start creating chords all we do is start using combinations of notes to create a chord.

Definition of a chord: 3 or more notes played together.

Each chord has its own formula, expressed as numbers, being Roman Numerals or English Numbers.

The Formula for a Major Chord is I III V, or 1 3 5.

So, to create a C-Major Chord, we take the 1st, 3rd and the 5th notes of the C-Major scale and we have a C-Major Chord.

Can you work out the notes from the scale above?

They are **C, E and G.**

Right then, let's have a look and the chord of C that we've already learned and check the notes.

C-Major

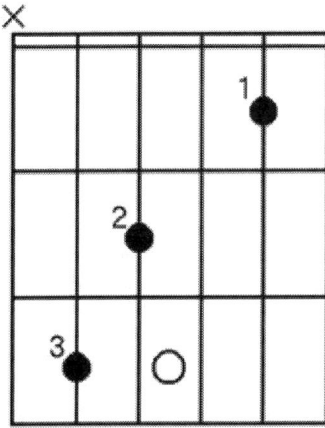

Let's go through the Chord String by String

6th String = NOT PLAYED

5th String = C

4th String = E

3rd String = G

2nd String = C

1st String = E

So, as you can see, all the notes that we have been playing are part of the chord that we created above from our theory. Notice also that C and E are repeated. This is normal and is part of the way we play the guitar to give the chord a richer sound than it would if we only played the three we had to.

Let's try and do it backwards now.

Here is the chord of G Major that we have been playing.

Let's use the Note Diagram from Page 1 and write out the notes that we are actually playing.

G-Major

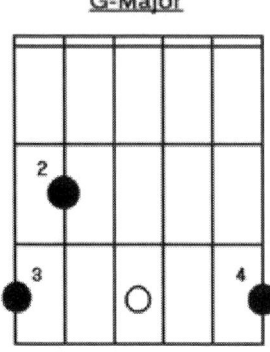

6th String = G
5th String = B
4th String = D
3rd String = G
2nd String = B
1st String = G

So now we quickly write out the notes for the G-Major scale and apply our 1, 3, 5 formula and get the notes from our theory.

G	A	B	C	D	E	F#	G
1	2	3	4	5	6	7	Oct

1, 3, 5 = G, B and D

Does it match the notes we have been playing?

Test Yourself Now

Here's a D-Major Scale.

D	E	F#	G	A	B	C#	D
1	2	3	4	5	6	7	Oct

SOME QUESTIONS TO TEST

1. Work out the notes of the D-Major chord by theory.
2. Now work out what you play.
3. Do they match?
4. Does it matter that the D note is played twice?
5. On your own, work out the notes for an A-Major Chord.
6. Now do an E-Major Chord.
7. Now try an F-Major Chord.

VIDEO ACCOMPANIMENT IS AVAILABLE FOR THIS LESSON

Head to http://learnguitar.nz

LESSON 3 – MINOR CHORDS

Of course, we've been playing all sorts of chords with interesting names and interesting sounds. They all have their own formula just like the Major chord we have done previously.

<u>We'll start with the Minor Chord.</u>

Okay, the formula is simple. All you do is flatten the 3rd.

So it reads:

I bIII V, or 1 flat3, 5

Can you work out the notes for C-Minor?

C	D	E	F	G	A	B	C
1	2	3	4	5	6	7	Oct

1 = C

flat3 = Eb

5 = G

So let's create an open chord version of Cm, now that we know the notes are C, Eb and G.

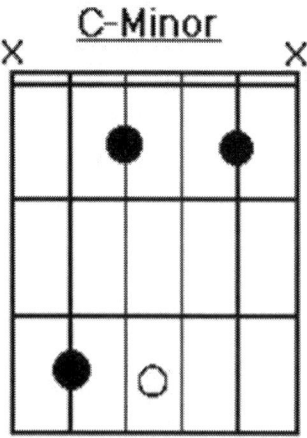

So let's have a look at the chord

Both the 6th string and the 1st string are muffled. This is because as open notes they are E, when the C-Minor chord has an Eb note. They are not part of the chord and should not be played!

- So we have the C note on the 5th string and the 2nd string. That is our I
- The Eb note is on the 4th string. That's our III
- The G note is on the 3rd string. That is our V

So there is actually nothing difficult about creating this chord. It's quite tricky to play however, so whether you use it or would prefer to stick to the Barre Chord is entirely a matter of taste!

Test yourself now.

Write out the notes for the following chords.

Gm =

Am =

B =

Em =

A =

Fm =

Did you get them all right?

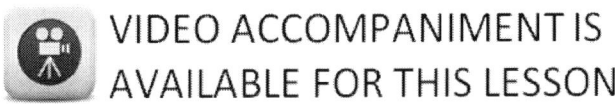 VIDEO ACCOMPANIMENT IS AVAILABLE FOR THIS LESSON

Head to http://learnguitar.nz

LESSON 4 – SEVENTHS & MAJOR-SEVENTHS

Dominant Seventh

When we play a chord like E7, we are in effect playing an Edominant7th, just shortened to E7. This is standard, and we will continue to refer to E7 as E7, but just a note of its real name.

The formula for a Dominant 7th (or 7th) is quite simple: **I, III, V, bVII or 1 3 5 flat7**

As you may have noticed, it's the notes or the Major chord, with an added note being the flattened seventh. This gives the 7th note a dominant tone and hence a dominant name.

The notes for the C7 are then **C E G and Bb**

Check this against the actual chord we have been playing and make sure they are right.

Now by yourself work out the notes of the A7, D7 and E7 and check them against what we've been playing.

Are they all correct?

Major-Seventh

This formula is even simpler. The seventh note in this is just the 7th straight from the Major scale with no flattening or sharpening.

The formula is: **I III V VII, or 1 3 5 7**

Work out the notes and chord shapes for the chords below and write them into blank chord box diagrams.

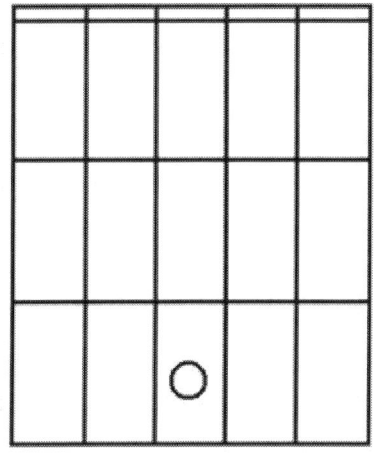
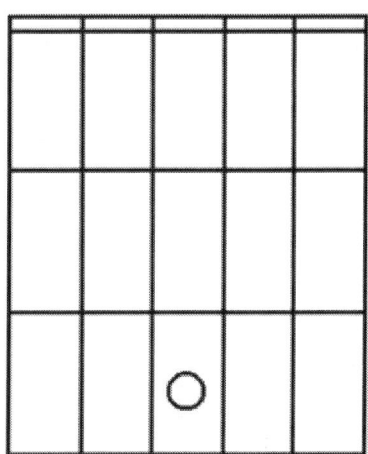

VIDEO ACCOMPANIMENT IS AVAILABLE FOR THIS LESSON

Head to http://learnguitar.nz

LESSON 5 – MINOR-SEVENTHS

We all play them, but how about where they come from.

Simple formula, like the Minor Chord, being I bIII V, but with a bVII added on.

So the formula is: **I bIII V bVII, or 1 flat3 5 flat7**

Here is the notes for an Am7 chord: A C E G

Work out a Dm7, Fm7, Em7, Bm7 and write the results into some blank chords diagrams like the ones below.

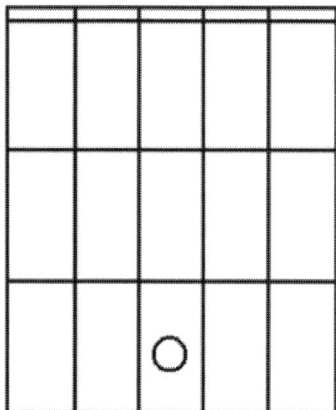 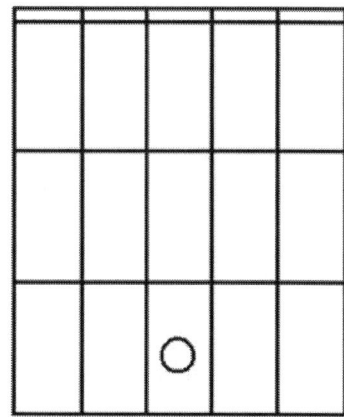

Head to http://learnguitar.nz

LESSON 6 - USING OUR CHORD CONSTRUCTION FOR SONGS

When you play a song or a piece of music, most of the time (99.99%) you are playing in a certain key, whatever that key may be.

There are 12 different keys for the twelve different notes, with Major and Minor – in effect 24 different keys.

For now, we'll concentrate on the Major keys, coming from the Major scales that we have already learned how to create.

Let's stick with C.

Remember how in the beginners course, you learned how to work out the chords of a key by another formula?

The formula was:

Major Minor Minor Major Major Minor Diminished Major

So quite simply the chords of the key of C-Major are

C Dm Em F G Am Bdim C

With this lesson, we'll learn why those are the chords for C-Major.

Let's look at the notes of our C-Major Scale.

C D E F G A B C

Now, let's work out the 1 3 5 starting from each note of the C-Major scale.

To do this, we use the notes from our C-Major Scale.

Example, the first letter of our scale is C. So the 1 3 5 from that note is **C E G.**

The second letter is D. So the 1 3 5 from that note is **D F A.**

Do you understand?

Let's finish it off.

	C	D	E	F	G	A	B	C
I	C	D	E	F	G	A	B	C
III	E	F	G	A	B	C	D	E
V	G	A	B	C	D	E	F	G

These are called TRIAD'S. TRI meaning 3, and they always follow a 1, 3, 5 pattern.

So a triad beginning on the note of D, and in the Key of C-Major, has the notes D, F and A.

A TRIAD starting from the note of G, and in the key of C-Major, has the notes G, B and D.

Do you understand how we create Triad's from within the Major Scale?

So let's go back to our Table of notes.

	C	D	E	F	G	A	B	C
I	C	D	E	F	G	A	B	C
III	E	F	G	A	B	C	D	E
V	G	A	B	C	D	E	F	G

It is made up of triads.

Triads also form our chords as we learned in the last lesson.

Take a look at the notes.

C, E, and G are the notes of the first triad. They are also the notes of the C-Major Chord, being the 1st, 3rd and 5th of the C-Major Scale.

The next triad has the notes of D, F, and A. So if we have a look at the D-Major scale, we see that the notes are the I bIII and V

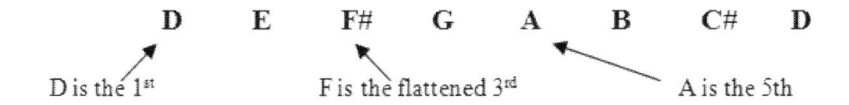

```
         D      E     F#      G      A      B     C#     D
         ↑             ↑                    ↑
    D is the 1st   F is the flattened 3rd      A is the 5th
```

So if our triad is 1 flat3 and 5, then it is a Minor Chord. The second triad of the C-Major scale is a Dm chord.

Now, if we do the rest, we find that they follow our pattern of:

Major Minor Minor Major Major Minor Diminished Major

The only one which we haven't learned to identify is the Diminished Chord.

Can you work out the formula?

Here is a B-Major Scale

B C# D# E F# G# A# B

We know the notes are B D and F in the key of C-Major.

The I III V from this scale is B D# and F#.

So if we flatten the 3rd and the 5th, we have our triad.

It is called a Diminished Triad, or dim when written in chord format.

Now, how to play a diminished chord?

Well, by now you may well have noticed that in playing our guitar, we are playing lots of different shapes with our left hand for lots of different chords. One way or another, these shapes are all related back to our triads. So the diminished triad or chord is no different. Just another shape.

Playing a Dimished Chord

Here is the shape of a standard Diminshed Chord.

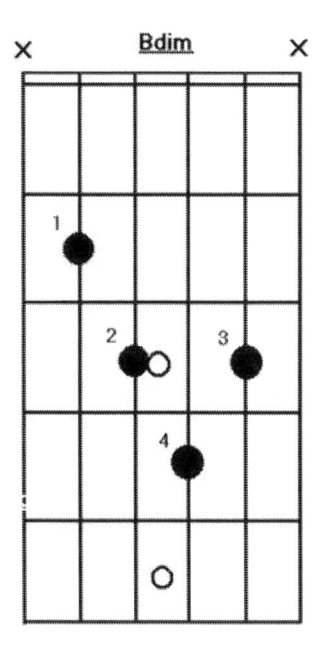

- See that the B note is here on the second string.
- It is the same root notes as that which we use for our A-Shape Barre chords.
- So, in effect, we could easily add this shape to out A-Shape Barre Chord shapes.
- Take note also that the 1st and the 6th strings are not played.

Okay, do you have it quite clear about triads and how they are used to create our chords, and how they come from our major scales.

We now know that each Major Key, being has it's own set of chords, and we can work out these chords quite simply by writing out the major scale and then applying the formula to it.

What about Minor Scales and Keys?

Many, many, songs are written in minor keys. Minor key's have a mournful sad sound, contrasting the Major key's happy-go-lucky type of sound and feel. Minor Key's are simple and easy to work out as well.

The first we will do is called the Natural Minor.

VIDEO ACCOMPANIMENT IS AVAILABLE FOR THIS LESSON

Head to http://learnguitar.nz

LESSON 7 – NATURAL MINOR SCALES

In any major scale, the sixth note VI is said to be the Relative minor.

By being a relative minor they share the same notes and chords.

We'll once again write out our C-Major Scale.

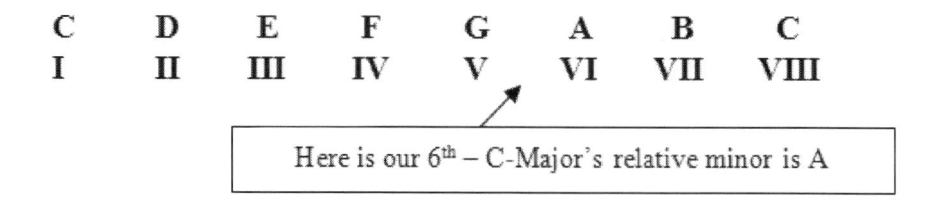

C	D	E	F	G	A	B	C
I	II	III	IV	V	VI	VII	VIII

Here is our 6th – C-Major's relative minor is A

The Sixth is A. So using the notes of the C-Major scale, we can now create an A-minor scale.

A B C D E F G A

Create a D-Major Scale now.

D E F# G A B C# D

What's the relative minor?

Answer: **Bm**

Easy, right?

There is also a formula (there always is a another formula!!!), and it goes

Whole   Half   Whole   Whole   Half   Whole   Whole

So using our new formula, can you create an B-Minor scale?

B C D E F G A B

The first gap has to be a W, so we have to raise the C to C#, the next gap is now from C# to D which is a half step and OK.

The next is D to E which is whole and OK. The next is E to F, which is half when it needs to be whole, so we raise the F to F#. F# to G is OK at half. G to A is OK at whole. And A to B is OK at whole.

So here are the notes of a Bm scale.

B C# D E F# G A B

Are they the same as the D-Major Scale?

Natural Minor Scale Triads

So we know what the notes of a natural minor scale are. What about the triads and then the chords?

Let's look at A-minor, the relative minor to C-Major.

A B C D E F G A

Now we do the table for the I III V setup.

	A	B	C	D	E	F	G	A
I	A	B	C	D	E	F	G	A
III	C	D	E	F	G	A	B	C
V	E	F	G	A	B	C	D	E

Let's look at the triad's and see what chords they make.

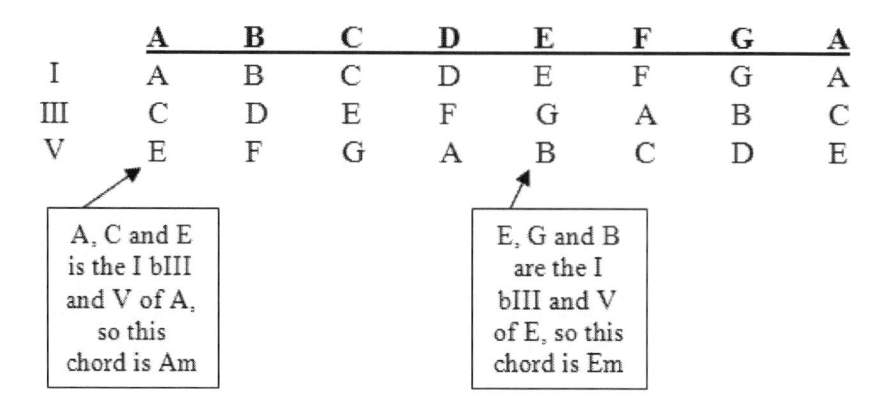

	A	B	C	D	E	F	G	A
I	A	B	C	D	E	F	G	A
III	C	D	E	F	G	A	B	C
V	E	F	G	A	B	C	D	E

A, C and E is the I bIII and V of A, so this chord is Am

E, G and B are the I bIII and V of E, so this chord is Em

Can you can work out the rest for yourself?

Here are all the answers for the key of A Minor.

Am Bdim C Dm Em F G Am

So for the chords of a Natural minor scale, they are

Minor Diminished Major Minor Minor Major Major Minor

Now, for yourself work out the triads and chords for the keys of Bm and Em.

Write your answers on a sheet of paper.

As a further exercise, write next to all the main Major Keys, the relative minor's of each different key.

Major Key	Relative Minor
C	
D	
E	
F	
G	
A	
B	

VIDEO ACCOMPANIMENT IS AVAILABLE FOR THIS LESSON

Head to http://learnguitar.nz

LESSON 8 – SONG CONSTRUCTION

Using Your Theory and Knowledge of Chords to write songs

- So what's the trick to writing a good song?
- How do we find that great catch?
- Is there a formula for catchy songs?

The answer to the questions above is no.

There is no secret to writing songs that can be shared. The standard quote that rotates around about song writing is that a good song is 10% inspiration and 90% hard work.

This is quite true, and while we can never teach you the inspiration part, we can certainly show you where the hard work begins and maybe where it ends.

To write songs, inspiration aside, there are certain rules that apply.

For example in any key, there are the Basic Chords that we base everything else around. These chords are the 1st, the 4th and the 5th chords from the scale.

To be quite precise, the I IV V chord progression is the most played combination of chords in the music world. Literally millions of songs have been written using these three chords only.

Let's look at a couple of examples.

12-Bar Blues - Uses E, A and B (I IV V of E)

Louie Louie - Uses A, D and E (I IV V of A)

There are thousands more; in fact entire song books for guitar have been released with I IV V combinations in them. They are the base chords, and have names as well.

I is the ROOT

IV is the SUB-DOMINANT

V is the DOMINANT

The next chord in popularity for use and inclusion into our song is the **VI**, or the **Relative** Minor. It's use is widespread for a bridge, or a lead break, or just a variation. It can also be easily included into the basic verse or chorus.

Other than that, the other chords can be included as a matter of taste, but the I IV V and VI are the most common and the easiest to work with.

Of course, you're free to include other chords that are out of key, or something completely off the wall, but that's personal tastes.

Flavouring

Not all songs are written using just Major and Minor chords, and that's where all our 7th's, add9's, sus 2's and 4's, sixth's and all the other different chords are used – they are flavouring over the basic idea. Standard Major and Minor chords can become boring and monotonous, so if you like the idea you've got, but want to add a little something to it, the first place to turn is to the FLAVOUR chords.

Applying our Theory on Scales, Triads, Chords and Songwriting

Basically to apply it, start writing!

It's easy to write songs, just hard to write really good songs like the audience demands these days.

What I've done here is put together a little piece of music and songwriting that begins to utilise all the things we have learned here. It'll take a bit of practice, and it's not all shown here, but the main riff is here, as well as the Chords for the Verse and the Chorus. Have a good look and a good play, but have a bit of an analysis to see what techniques are being used as well as how the chords relate back to our theory.

It's called **War, Bloody War**, and it's in the key of G Major.

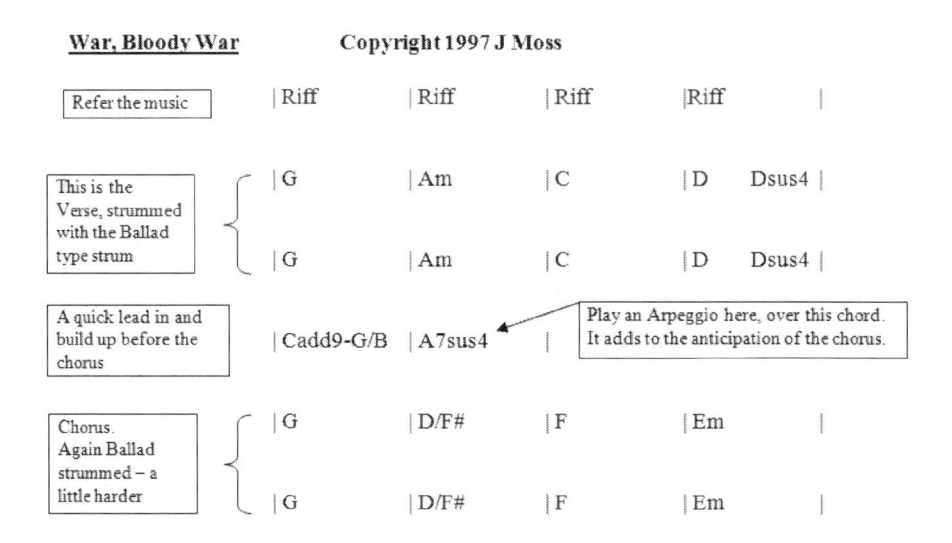

War, Bloody War   Copyright 1997 J Moss

Refer the music		Riff		Riff		Riff		Riff		
This is the Verse, strummed with the Ballad type strum		| G		| Am		| C		| D	Dsus4 |	
		| G		| Am		| C		| D	Dsus4 |	
A quick lead in and build up before the chorus		| Cadd9-G/B		| A7sus4		Play an Arpeggio here, over this chord. It adds to the anticipation of the chorus.				
Chorus. Again Ballad strummed – a little harder		| G		| D/F#		| F		| Em		|
		| G		| D/F#		| F		| Em		|

Below is the Main Riff

The chords are G and Cadd9, with the licks in the Em Pentatonic scale we have learned. If you hadn't already noticed, Em is the relative minor of G, which is the key we are playing in. This allows us to use the Em pentatonic to play in G if we wish.

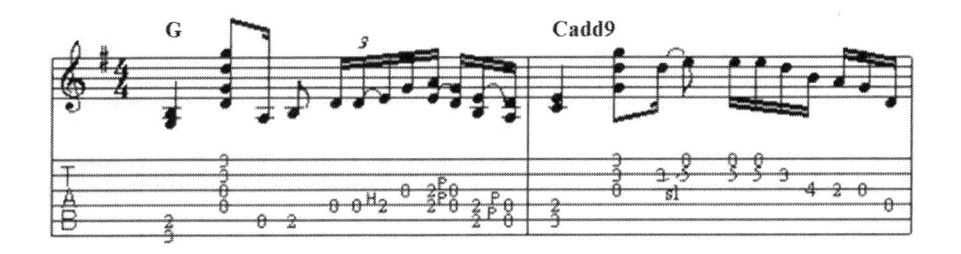

Songwriting and Structure

Of course, no song is a song without some form of structure.

There is no real set strictures on structure, but again like the others, there are the basics and the basis on which most (a darn lot!) of songs are structured, especially the modern Top40 type songs.

Most of these songs have a hook. The hook can double as an introduction and then get repeated as a bridge, or can just be the chorus. The hook can be a repeating riff a la Satisfaction by the Rolling Stones or Smoke on the Water by Deep Purple. Or the hook could be the lovely constructed verse that just flows and flows into the rest of the song. The hook could be the Structure itself a-la Stairway to Heaven by Led Zeppelin, where the structure just keeps the song building and building until an eventual climactic lead break and final verse.

Most of these songs have a simple structure. Usually based around a system:

Verse / Chorus / Verse / Chorus / Lead-Break / Chorus/ Chorus / End

Additions can be easily added to this, like a flashy introduction, repeated as a bridge before the Lead Break, or just a flashy bridge in a different key (for contrast).

Let's have a look at a classic structure for Top40 success.

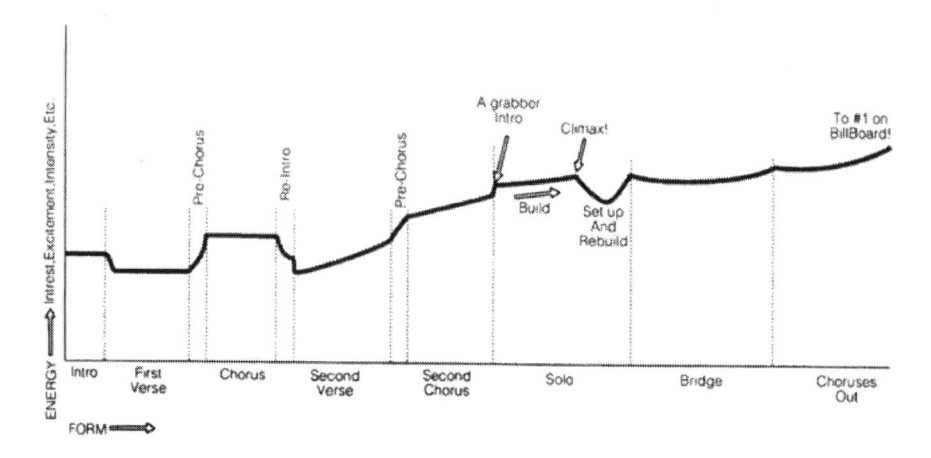

Graph showing song energy/interest over form sections:

- Y-axis: ENERGY / Interest, Excitement, Intensity, Etc.
- X-axis (FORM): Intro, First Verse, Chorus, Second Verse, Second Chorus, Solo, Bridge, Choruses Out
- Labels along the curve: Pre-Chorus, Re-Intro, Pre-Chorus, A grabber Intro, Build, Climax!, Set up And Rebuild, To #1 on BillBoard!

The graph is quite self-explanatory, and is concerned with not only the classic structure, being quite complex with all the additions that can be added without cluttering the song. (Take note: over-structured songs can easily become clumsy and the listener will lose interest very quickly.)

The other part of the graph of particular interest to us is the Y-Axis, being the energy line.

When we play a song, we don't play the whole thing with the same strum, or the same volume or the same emphasis on all parts of the song. We use different *techniques* that we have learned to add **tension** and **variation** to the song. For example, remember the strum work we did in the beginner's course with simple changes to our strum to completely change the tone of the song. Same with our more advanced song-writing techniques.

We want to build the song towards the climax, whether it be in the lead-break section as per the graph or somewhere else. This building idea is quite important, as we don't want to sound like the great Monotone Songwriter.

Anyway, let's analyse **War, Bloody War** and see what conclusions we can come up with.

From the beginning.

We have a 4 bar introduction, consisting of a riff over the I and the IV of the Key we are in. Chord I is of course the Root, while Chord IV, is one of the main three that we use predominantly. It is catchy, flows and varied with the length of the notes we play i.e. doesn't go just 1 2 3 4 5 6 7 8 9 etc etc. By repeating the two bars, we have solo guitar beginning the song, then second time through it gives the Drummer and Bass player a to come in, immediately starting to Build and Lift the song.

The Verse is an 8 Bar Phrase, consisting of two repeated 4 bar phrases. These are strummed lightly in the background, giving the vocalist his/her chance to establish himself/herself and set the tone for the lyrics.

The Pre-Chorus, is as per the graph. Two bars with which to set things up to go into the chorus nicely. The last chord is an A7sus4, which is a great flavour chord, and leads into the G for the chorus very well. To set the tone for the chorus and provide a variation we play a simple arpeggio over this chord instead of strummed. This appears to slacken the pace of the song before we wind up to chorus.

The Chorus, like the Verse, is an 8 bar Phrase, using a repeated 4 bar phrase. We use a different theory in this part of the song, which changes the feel and tone again, flavouring the chorus. The chords are G D/F# F and Em. If you haven't already noticed, F is out of key. The chord works however, because we are styling a different idea – a descending bass line. The first chord is G, which has a G bass. The second is D/F#, which has an F# bass note. The third chord is F, with an F bass, and the fourth Em, with an E bass. The chorus works in this instance because of the Chromatically descending bass line i.e. going down a half-step at a time. It begins to sound like a slow walk down some stairs.

And where to from here? After the Chorus, we play the pre-chorus again, which leads us back to the intro (notice that the Chorus and the Intro both start on G, so the A7sus4 leads really well into both Chorus and Intro). After that we repeat everything, and then we're ready for the Bridge (if there is one!) and the lead break (again, if there is one!), before we would repeat the chorus and fade out.

We will leave you there to practice and enjoy, and we'll work on the lead break for this song in a couple of weeks.

Good luck and good playing – oh, and good writing too!

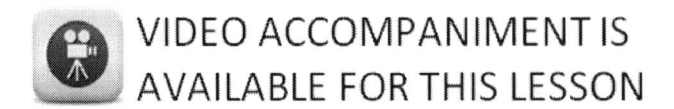

VIDEO ACCOMPANIMENT IS AVAILABLE FOR THIS LESSON

Head to http://learnguitar.nz

SESSION 3

In this session, we're going to cover a bit of theory, a bit of exercises, a couple of interesting pieces, and a lot of playing.

We're going to be learning a lot of different techniques, both left hand and right, and we'll be learning to apply these into the songs and pieces of music that we play.

To accomplish this, we need to continue to train our hands and minds to do what we wish. For this reason, we need exercises to continue this training. The most basic of these is SCALES. To date, we've learned how to do a Minor Pentatonic in any key scale and also a C-Major scale in the open position. The Minor Pentatonic is a scale, that while it still needs to be practiced to be learnt, doesn't need the kind of attention that we'll be giving the C-Major. You see, the C-Major is a scale that we use for exercise, while at this stage the Minor Pentatonic is a scale that we will use parts of to do our licks and fills within the songs or pieces. The Chromatic scale, of course, is also an exercise scale.

There are also myriad's of other techniques that are going to need work and practice. What we'll be doing is learning the technique and then putting it to practice in a short piece or exercise. While long, full length songs sound great, it is very difficult to implement all the different techniques at once, or consistently. For this reason, these exercises must be approached with serious thoughts in mind, in view of being able to do them consistently well every time. It won't happen at once, and some even may continue to elude perfection for months. But only after we know them inside out and backwards do they start coming into our playing in a natural manner. If you don't know them, they will sound forced, and ultimately you would have been better off playing them the same way you always had and keeping the song flowing.

Anyway, enough! Let's get on with it.

LESSON 1 – SCALES

You should now be familiar with C-Major Scale Pattern 1.

Below you will see C-Major Scale Pattern 2. These two scales, and the others which will be coming in the forthcoming lessons, are for exercise. We don't have a great deal of practical use for them just at the moment, which is unlike everything else that we have been shown, but they are for exercise.

With regard to being exercise, the techniques we employ to play them must be precise. If you haven't already done so, your right hand should be consistently using a Up/Down/Up/Down/ Up/Down/Up/Down motion. Check to make sure that this is what is actually happening. Watch yourself play Pattern 1 a couple of times, concentrating only on the RIGHT hand. If you are making a couple of downstrokes in a row, or a couple of up, slow it down and concentrate on getting the picking correct.

With the left hand and our Chromatic Scale, we've been pushing the technique for 1-Finger-Per-Fret. This is how we will continue to play as we move up and down the fretboard. It is important that we maintain this position for our left hand, and in fact, with the guitar, this is called POSITION PLAYING. Scales such as Pattern 1 are said to be in the OPEN position, but Pattern 2 below is in a different POSITION. We move our 1st finger up to the 2nd Fret. Our 2nd finger plays all notes on the 3rd fret, our 3rd finger all notes on the 4th fret, and our 4th finger all notes on the 5th fret. In effect 1 finger per-fret from which ever fret be being. It is the fret we begin on that tells us what the position is. For example, Pattern 2 is in the second position, so our 1st finger takes place on the second fret, with the other fingers up from there.

As you can see, Pattern 2 has two notes which don't fit our Position. These are the notes on the 1st fret of the sixth and first string. To play these notes, we move our 1st finger back to play them. What we DO NOT do is move the whole of our left hand in order to play these notes! It is important to keep our POSITION, and for notes such as this, we only need to move a single finger a little out of position, and NOT the whole hand.

Time to learn the scale. Remember to play it slowly and smoothly. Try to keep it coordinated all the way through, and don't be tempted to tear up and down the scale as fast as you can manage. It's much better to play at a comfortable speed and play accurately.

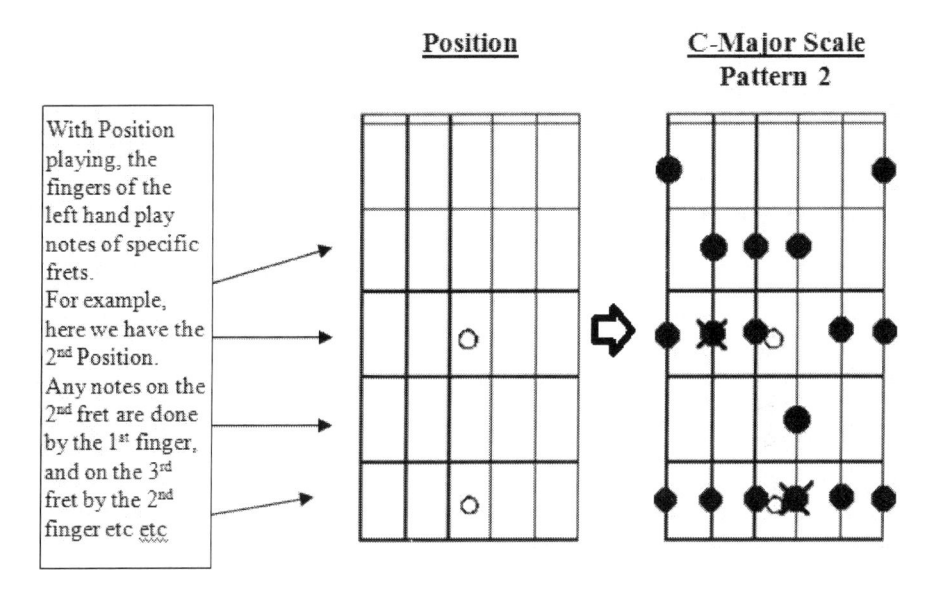

Position

C-Major Scale Pattern 2

With Position playing, the fingers of the left hand play notes of specific frets. For example, here we have the 2nd Position. Any notes on the 2nd fret are done by the 1st finger, and on the 3rd fret by the 2nd finger etc etc

For your practice and daily warmup, you should use scales.

Play the Chromatic about 20 times daily, then do each of the Major Scales 10 times each ascending and descending. When you reach the end of your daily practice, you should do the same again as a 'warmdown'.

With this, you will notice daily improvements to your scales, and then after a little while, improvements to your technique which will help you playing.

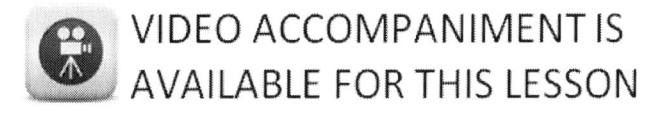

VIDEO ACCOMPANIMENT IS AVAILABLE FOR THIS LESSON

Head to http://learnguitar.nz

LESSON 2 – A RETURN TO THE BLUES

Blues music is a great to way to learn about Rhythm and Phrasing, and as well as all this learning taking place, you get to play some great music as we go.

To have reached this point, we should be competent at playing the Shuffle Rhythm with open chords; i.e. the E-E6-E7-E6 and simile on A. We should also be able to apply a slide on the B7, or an A7 slide up and down a fret. If you're doing well, then you should be able to apply the turnaround lick in those last two bars of the twelve bars.

Basically, it should sound pretty good already.

But we can certainly keep going and add a little more.

To play the blues with the feel and emotion that it deserves, it's best if we know a little more about it first before we carry on.

Here's a few facts explained.

- Blues is a Shuffle type Rhythm, with a bit of a groove and a bit of extra feel that cannot even be passed off to being a Groove.
- It's in 4/4 time, being Four beats to the bar, but the timing is always a little out. It can't be divided into eighth notes and sixteenth notes, and so often gets put into triplets, but even this still isn't strictly correct.
- Sometimes Blues gets written as 12/8 time, which in effect is 4/4 time using triplets. Even still, blues is always written with anecdotes like "Play with Swing" or "Use Shuffle" – Either way, it's still saying that there is no real way to account for that Blues feel on paper. Just so you know, see the examples below.

The example below is in 12/8 time (see the Time Signature to the far left), which means to play 12 Eighth notes. With the rest in the middle of each group of three, it gives the Clip-itty-Clop feel well.

The example below is in normal 4/4 time, using eighth and sixteenth notes to try and portray the blues shuffle feel. Is technically and mathematically incorrect for blues music and will have lots of anecdotes to try and give the shuffle impression.

The example below is about as close as I think we can accurately get to transcribing blues music onto paper. It's in 4/4 and since blues definitely has 4 beats to the bar, this is correct. As with the others, is still not quite spot-on and will have anecdotes to add shuffle and swing.

What are we going to do with this?

Blues based Rhythm Work.

Blues music is a terrific way to develop your rhythm and playing in time with different values on notes. In the Beginner's Courses we learned how to play a shuffle rhythm using the open chords of E, E6 and E7, as well as A, A6 and A7. Now we're going to change these to Power Chord equivalents. Both are still Blues Shuffle Rhythms; one is just open chords and powerful, the other 'down and dirty' using low bass strings for a chunky sort of a rhythm.

With the beginners course, there wasn't much mention made about swing rhythms and the like, instead just a bit of pressure for the chord changing. What we've got below is a couple of bars of the Power Chord Shuffle in E – the first one is arranged in a straight rhythm with no shuffle, the second using my favourate of the three ways of transcribing Blues Rhythms onto paper. The TAB will tell you that there really isn't a great deal of difference in them in playing, it's just the timing (or interpretation of it) that is different.

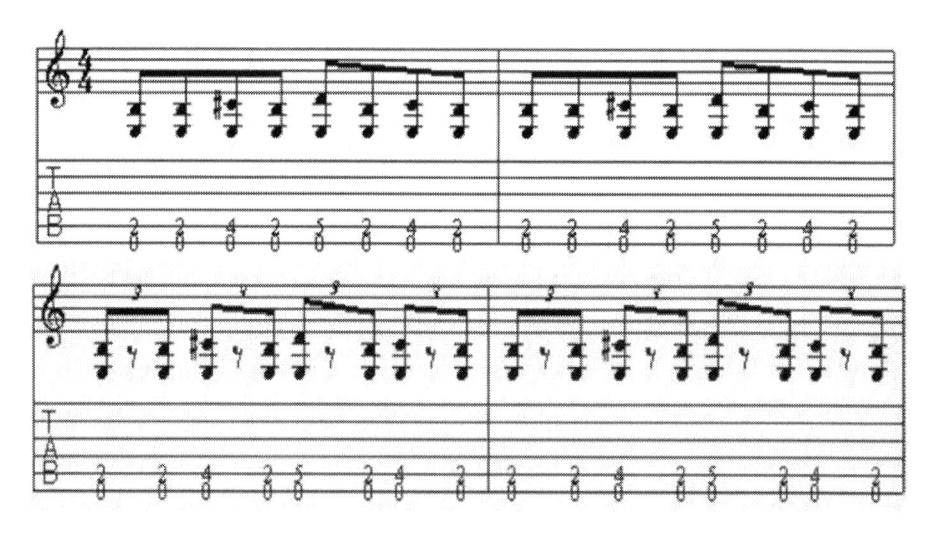

So, as you can see (play) the left hand does nothing different for each of them than a change of timing.

What now?

Now we add to them.

We're going to play our standard shuffle, but we're going to add a little riff.

Here is the Riff.

Effectively, what we have here is a Shuffle/Triplet/Shuffle/Triplet/ etc etc based riff.

This makes is easy for us to play as the right hand stays exactly the same – with the Right Hand playing a consistent rhythm, the left can quite easily cope with the hammer-on triplet lick.

Below is a few bars for you to practice with. Check out the change to the A. It's identical, just across the 5th and 4th strings instead of the 6th and 5th.

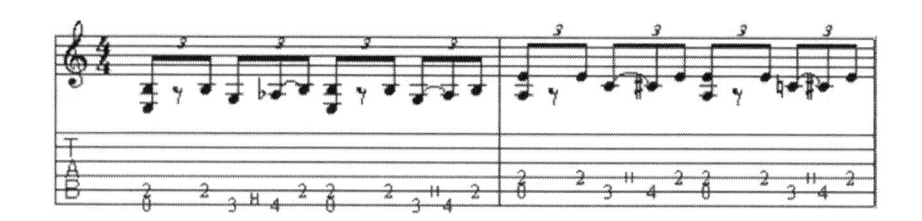

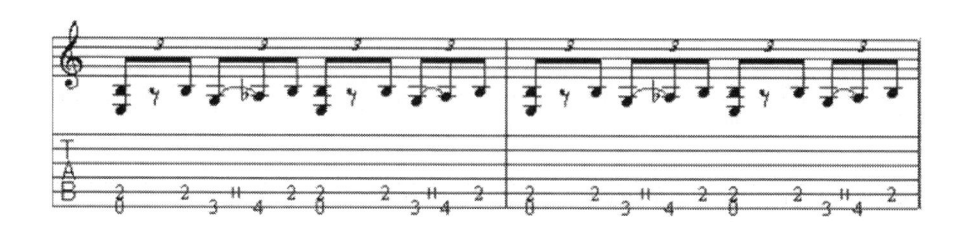

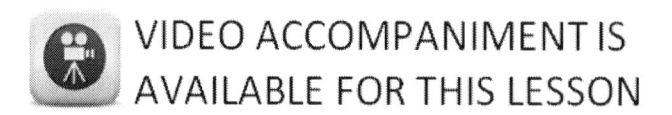

VIDEO ACCOMPANIMENT IS AVAILABLE FOR THIS LESSON

Head to http://learnguitar.nz

LESSON 3 – FINGERPICKING

As we all know, Fingerpicking is a wonderful and exciting way to play your guitar, no matter the style of music you prefer, and better yet, it sounds great to anybody listening to you play.

We've already covered basic fingerpicking patterns, and simple Arpeggio-style fingerpicking over a chord progression or song.

With this lesson, we're going to introduce you to a slightly different style of fingerpicking, where we start to pick a bit of a melody as well as the chordal backing. It's better suited to instrumentals at the moment, but is used to great effect during pauses in songs when the singer stops or takes a break, or for a fingerpicking lead-solo.

There are a few techniques we're going to learn to do this.

The most basic technique we will employ will be hammer-on and pull-off's.

Try and do the hammer-on/pull-off lick over a D chord as below, using the sus4 for the hammer-on/pull-off.

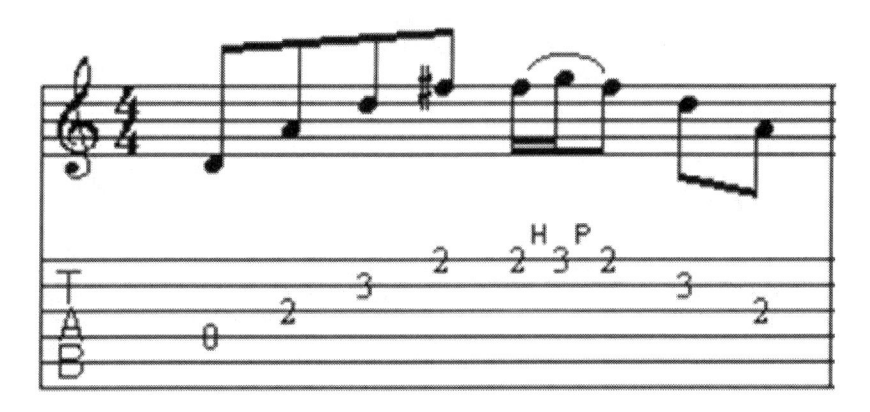

Now we're going to take that piece and add a little 'guts' to it – that is fatten it up a little. It sounds too much like single string plucking, so with a couple of simple changes, it will fill in nicely. We'll still keep the main theme (the h-on/p-off lick) intact though.

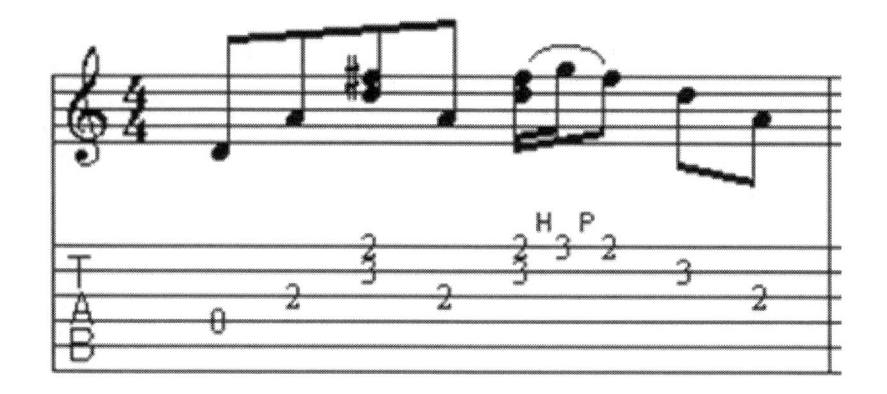

Can you hear the difference? It's always a matter of taste as to whether you like it or not, but by plucking 2 strings at once, we really filled in the chord – fattened it up!

This is a technique we can use. Straight fingerpicking patterns can become thin if used too much, and this is an easy way to add a bit of fill without too much effort. Try it on some other chords now; how about Asus4?

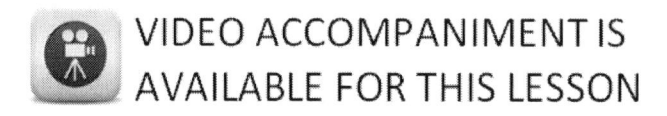

VIDEO ACCOMPANIMENT IS AVAILABLE FOR THIS LESSON

Head to http://learnguitar.nz

LESSON 4 – ARPEGGIO WORK

Arpeggio's are a lovely way to play the guitar. Their rich tone and sharp sound gives a real energy to the instrument. They're not difficult either, just a little work with the right hand picking, with articulate left hand fingering and they practically leap off the fretboard.

Arpeggio's can also benefit from unusual fingerings and exotic chords. Flavour chords (ninths, elevenths, add9's, sus chords, inverted triads etc) can add an element of mystery, additional tones over the chord really enhance how they sound.

To begin with, we'll do a couple of exercises with right hand, a couple of patterns as such to use.

Study the ideas below and try to practice them over several chords.

The examples have been given using a G major chord.

The arpeggio below is a very common one. With chords that cover all six strings, it has a wonderful, rich and deep sound. On four string chords, a repeat of the note on the 1st string is played.

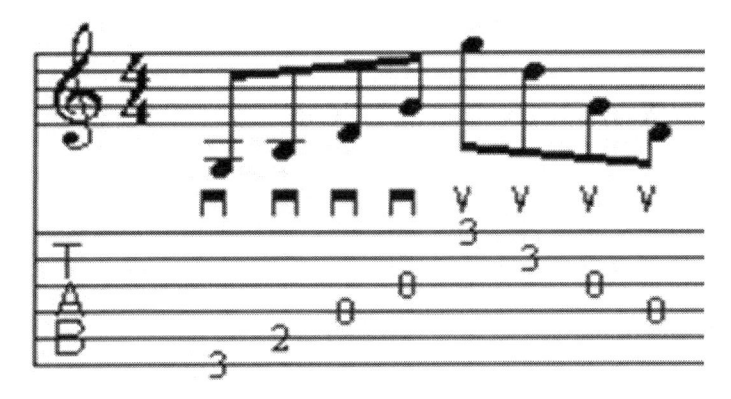

This one has quite a different sound, being slightly higher pitched. It's a bit different for the right hand, but make sure that you get the picking exact. Practice it enough so that it starts to feel natural to put the second downstroke in where we do.

This one is different again, and with the repeated bass and higher treble notes in the second half of the bar, has an almost pedal tone.

Very exciting style to use, especially when playing a piece a little faster.

This is simple to play, and offers no great variation that a little change in the timing.

The curved line over the top of the two notes means to "hold and play". In effect we pause for a ½ beat and let the note ring. This effect gives the music a chance to "breathe" in amongst the flurry of notes that arpeggios can seem to give the impression of.

VIDEO ACCOMPANIMENT IS AVAILABLE FOR THIS LESSON

Head to http://learnguitar.nz

LESSON 5 – MORE WORK FOR THE LEFT HAND.

Just to make things always interesting, we're going to do a little work on theory and chord construction.

As we know, we start the chord with our basic TRIAD, being a **I III V**.

We've already learned about 7ths and minor7th's, but now let's have a look at other chords.

The most common is the **add9**.

To create this chord, all we have to do is take a basic **I III V and literally add the 9**.

So for C, we've got C E and G, and now, if you count through the entire C-Major scale, and when you get back to the C again, call it 8. Continuing on, the next note is a D, which is also our 9. So for a Cadd9 chord, we use the notes of **C E G and D.**

Of course, how you play this chord is up to you. Below are a couple of examples of a Cadd9. Play them both; decide for yourself which one you like best. Of course, one might suit a particular song better than another, naturally, so don't be too rash in making a decision.

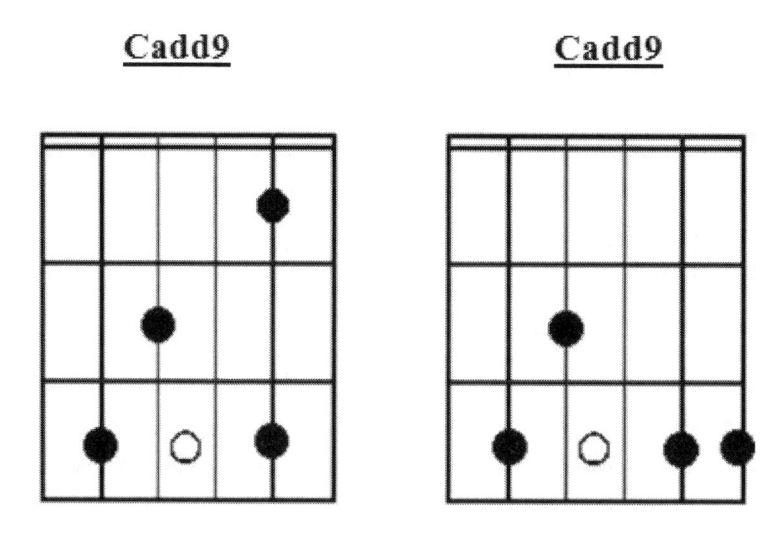

Cadd9

Cadd9

What about other add9 chords?

Well, the best ones are Cadd9, Aadd9, Eadd9, and although a bit tougher, Gadd9.

They all have that classic add9 feel which arpeggios love so much.

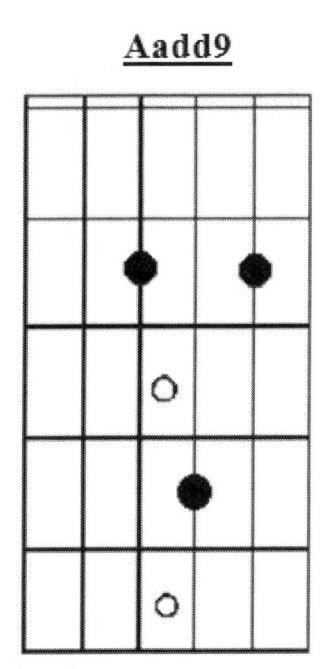

Aadd9

Gadd9

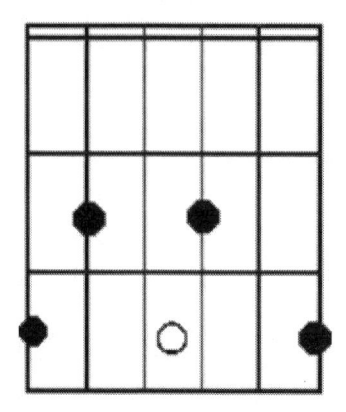

Eadd9

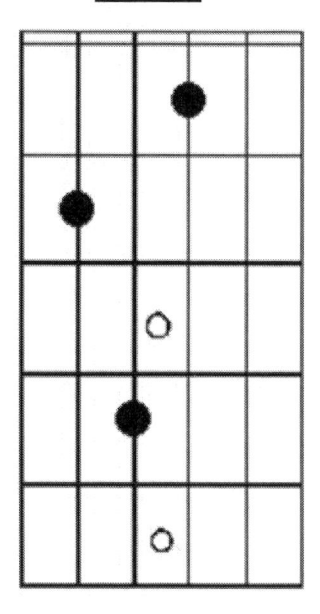

Another great technique is to change the BASS note away from the normal one we usually play.

For example, try playing a D chord and using the 5th string open (A) for a Bass. The A note is part of the D triad, so fits fine, and sounds good. Sounding even better is to make the bass note an F# as below.

If you do the D/F# with only three fingers and leave the 1st string open, the chord becomes a Dadd9/F#. This sounds even better.

Try other variations of triads, like A/C#, or G/B. They all have a place.

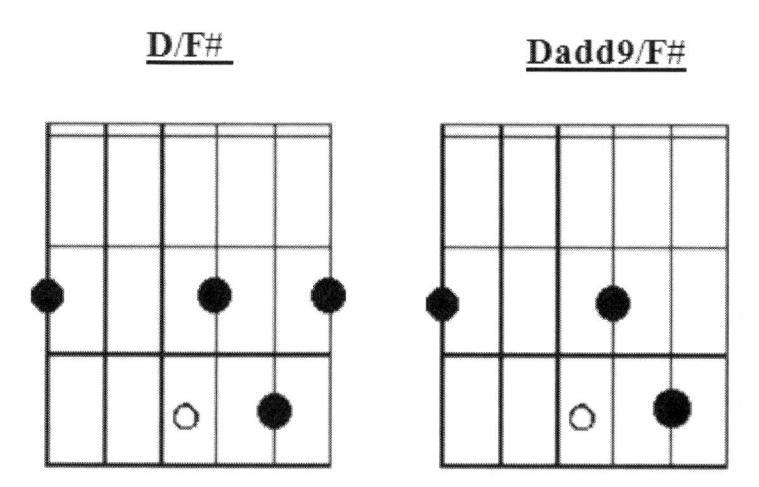

D/F#   **Dadd9/F#**

These are a type of inverted triads. Inverted meaning taking the I III V and changing it around slightly. This is not as predominant as on instruments such as the piano, as on the guitar we are restricted by fingerings. However, when playing inverted triads on the guitar, the tone is much richer and fuller.

Examples

Over the next page is a couple of short pieces that give examples of Arpeggio work. They use our standard chords, with a couple of add9's thrown in, and the odd inverted triad to show how the effect can work.

The chords are displayed for you, as are the chord progressions. There's no TAB for this, as it would be best if you experimented with each of the different Arpeggio patterns to see what you like best. Again, some will suit faster speeds, while other will sound richer with a slower pattern.

Have fun!

The First Example

This is a basic piece, with standard Left Hand Barre Chords. Play the E as an open chord, and the rest as Barre Chords.

| D/F#(add9) | G | A | Bm |

The Second Example

This piece uses Open chords exclusively, just different shapes that your left hand might take a little adjusting to get used to.

(Notice the different variation again on the D/F# chord.)

| A | E/G# | Asus2/F# | E | X 2 |
| A | A/C# | D/F# | D/E |

(Notice the different variation again on the D/F# chord.)

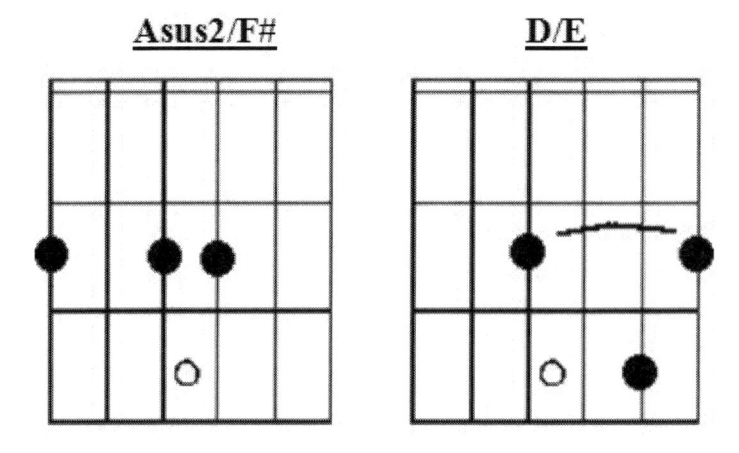

Asus2/F#   **D/E**

E/G#   **A/C#**

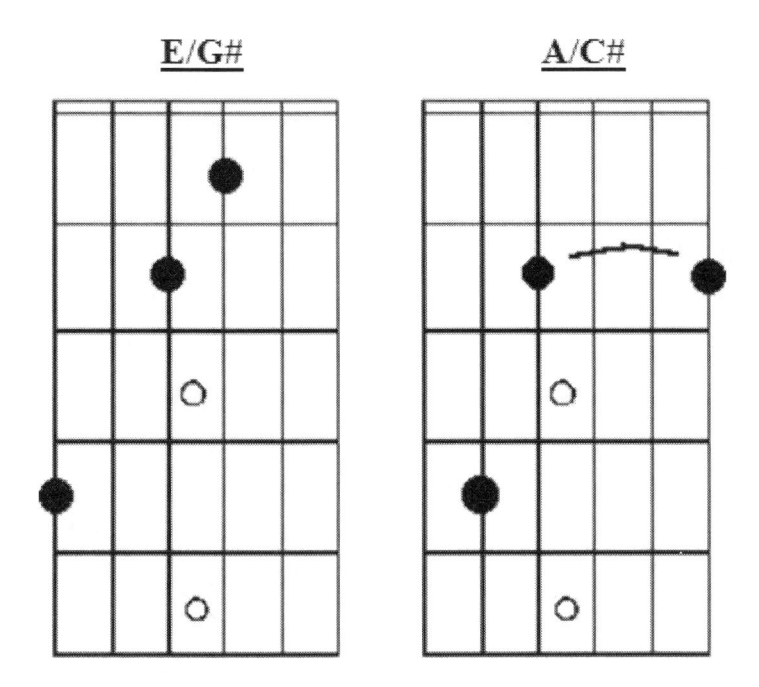

D/F#

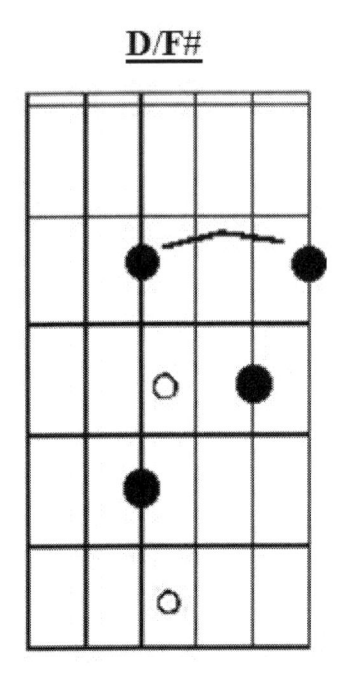

VIDEO ACCOMPANIMENT IS AVAILABLE FOR THIS LESSON

Head to http://learnguitar.nz

SESSION 4

Where are we going?

In this session, we're going to continue with the technique development and the exercises. We'll take our Arpeggios and improve on them a further, as we'll do the same with fingerpicking, with some really exciting ideas here.

We'll add another scale to our repertoire. We've got some great new ideas for riffs that will make a marked difference with our Blues Playing.

At the end of the lesson, is a bit more on the song we studied earlier. With War, Bloody War, we look at the structure and how the chorus and verses worked together, but we need a bridge or lead break in there. The last page is a lead break written exclusively so solo-guitar. Sounds great if played on an acoustic accurately.

Have fun.

LESSON 1 – C-MAJOR SCALE PATTERN 3

Here is the next scale in our continuing patterns. This one starts in the 5th position, and follows the 1-finger-per-fret system perfectly apart from the one note on the 4th string. As you can see, it is on the 10 fret. To play it, we stretch our little finger up to it without moveing the whole hand. This might feel quite difficult at first, but like the last scale pattern, it is important not to move the hand.

Remember also the rules of playing scales, and like the others, it applies here as well.

Here they are to refresh your memory.

1) Start at the lowest root note.

2) Ascend to the highest note in the scale.

3) Descend to the lowest note in the scale.

4) Return (if needed) to the lowest root note.

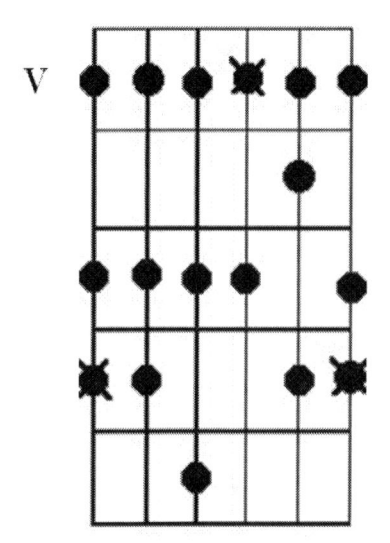

It's quite a stretch for the little finger to reach the 10th fret.

Persevere at it however, at it will begin to get easier.

Once again, remember that although it will feel difficult, keep trying at it won't take long.

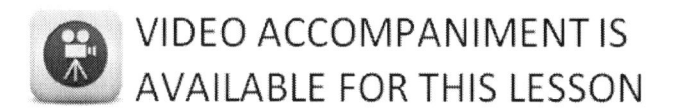

VIDEO ACCOMPANIMENT IS AVAILABLE FOR THIS LESSON

Head to http://learnguitar.nz

LESSON 2 – DEVELOPING THE BLUES SHUFFLE RHYTHM FURTHER.

As we learned last week about Triplets and their place in blues and swing music, we're going to do a continuation on that.

It's hard and takes a certain amount of Left Hand dexterity, but it's a really groovy line and if you get it right, sounds awesome.

Remember the E-E6-E7-E6 shuffle we did last week?

And do you remember the little Triplet riff we played over the E and A chords?

What we're going to do is blend the two together, add a quick triplet, and then a descending Bass line riff for a second bar – and suddenly we have a TWO bar blues based phrase.

Here is the first half of the first bar.

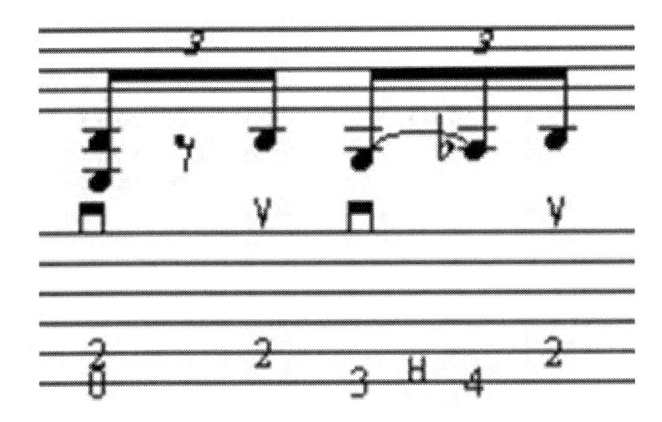

Here is the second half of the first bar.

Now we join them together.

You will find it quite handy however, to break it in half like this and to familiarise yourself with each before joining them.

Anyway, if you've done that, then lets join up.

First, let's look at what we know.

It's in 4/4 time, so four beats to the bar. It's made up of four groups of three notes - triplets. See the right hand picking – it is a consistent up/down – so there's nothing fancy in the right hand. Notice how the first two notes of the third beat are linked with the curved line. This is called a tie and means to hold them. We hold the note and so keep the right hand picking exactly the same. In the second beat, although we play the extra note, it's done with a Hammer-On, and so doesn't effect our right hand at all.

The Second Bar

This is really easy. Once again, we have exactly the same right hand motion, just a couple of changes for the left hand and we're away.

The left hand maintains position (2nd) until the very last beat.

Remember to keep the same shuffle rhythm.

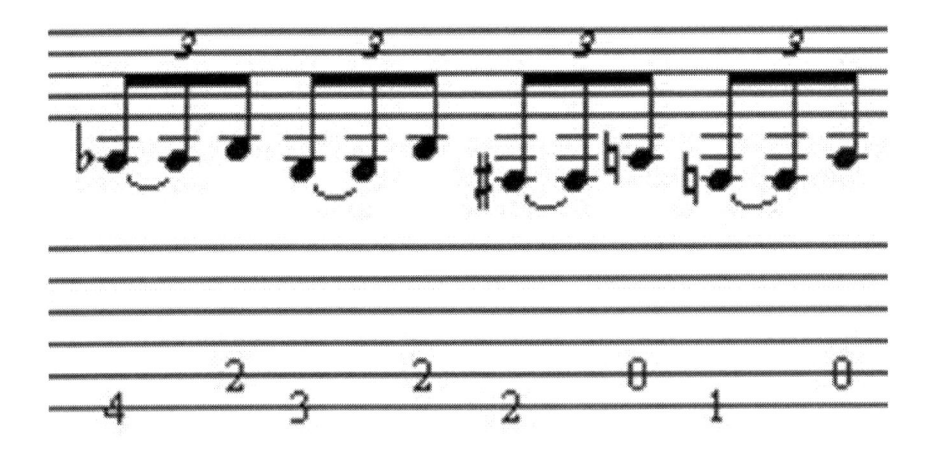

No problems?

Now let's put it together.

Here is the whole Two Bar Phrase.

So now, let's have a look at our 12 Bar Blues.

With the first line, we can either have four bars of E in a row, or the other popular standard of **E A E E**.

Naturally, our two bar phrase won't fit over the second, so we have to do the other.

So now, if we have four bars, we can play our riff twice. Great! But playing the same riff twice in a row can be bit boring. So lets do something different again.

The next bar is an A chord. So what if we designed a little riff to go from E to A. The simplest of these is to do a CHROMATIC ascending riff. For the last bar, what is we used our Power Chords and did a simple riff (still continuing to do the same right hand picking!) to take us to the A. The riff could use the chords E, F#, G and Ab, which is the chromatic ascent.

Here is the riff in TAB and music.

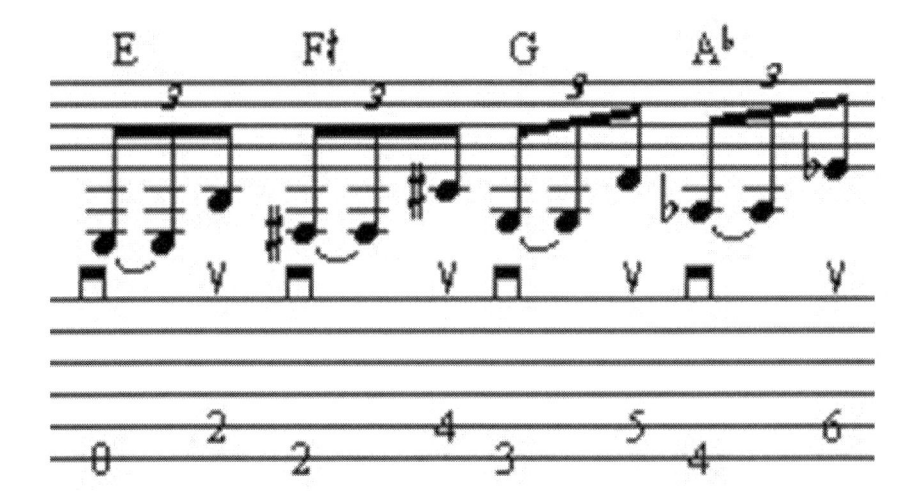

See how it takes the E to the A with a real groove?

Lets put it all together in the first four bars of our standard 12-Bar Blues.

Groovy stuff, now isn't it? Now try and put the same thing over the A chord.

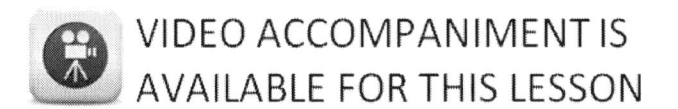

VIDEO ACCOMPANIMENT IS AVAILABLE FOR THIS LESSON

Head to http://learnguitar.nz

LESSON 3 – FINGERPICKING

So far with our fingerpicking to date, we've added in extras like the suspended chords and the occasional hammer-on and pull-off. We can apply the same with add9 chords, as well and changes from minor chords to minor sevenths, all of which add flavour to our playing.

Certainly the above ideas all improve our playing and take us outside the mould. But even still, we're still playing over chords, and merely enhancing them. But what about a true melody?

These are harder and more complex, but still just an addition to what we're already playing. Let's have a look at how we can start doing some melody-type playing.

Melody playing.

We'll start with the D chord, which is a nice easy one to play, and allows us the flexibility to show all the ideas.

Here is a basic fingerpicked bar of D, with a quick pull-off on the third beat.

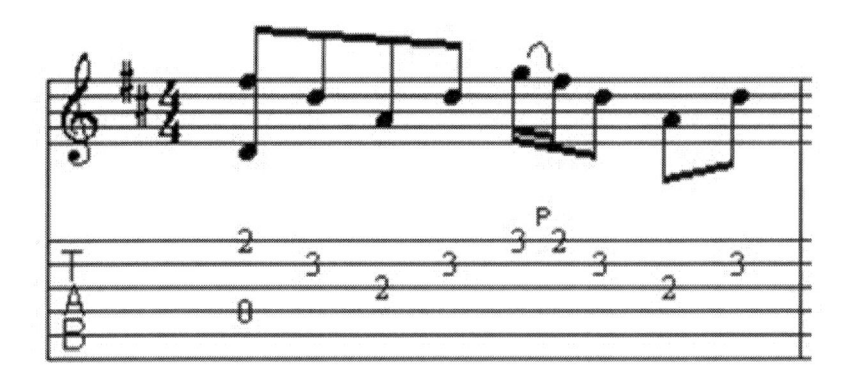

Now, while it might sound nice to be able to do away with playing over chord based rhythms altogether, that's not quite how it works. What we do is work the melody around the chords. It's also a much more fun way to play.

Now try this. Finger the D chord again, then play the below melody.

```
e|--2--2--0--2-----------3--------|
B|--3--3--3--3-----3--------------|
G|-----------------------------2--|
```

If playing this within the D chord, we're using the sus4 and sus2 chord, but we're also starting to play away from a simple arpeggio fingerpick.

Let's put the two together and make a two bar phrase.

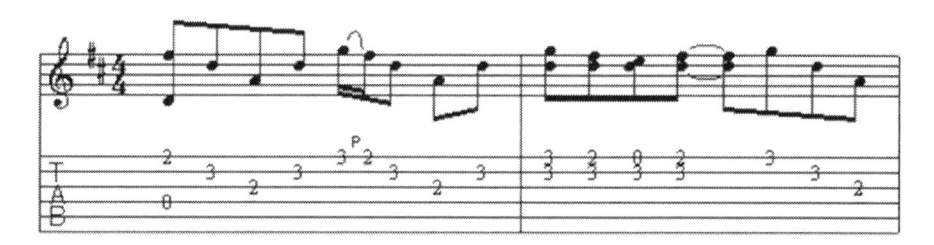

```
e|--------------3--2-----3--|--2--2--0--2-----------3--------|
B|--2--3--3--2-----3-----2--|--3--3--3--3-----3--------------|
D|--0-----------------------|-----------------------------2--|
```

Right then, see how we've taken a D-chord and really made it something.

Let's continue on the same lines.

How about this for a two bar phrase over C.

The first bar is along the same lines as the D, being arpeggio style with a quick hammer-on. The second bar is a little different again, using a slide and a bit more left hand technique. Work hard on getting the second bar smooth, with a legato-lick style playing style.

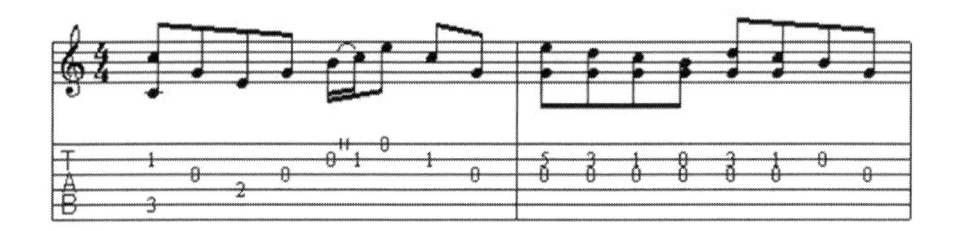

For exercise, take a couple of chord progressions and try and add some melody licks to them.

Take the two chords we've got above add a G to it, then back to D and we've got an 8 bar phrase.

Think of that as the verse of your song.

Now try to add a chorus (with melody fingerpicking) yourself. It's in the key of G, using the D chord as a starting chord, but the notes are still in the key of G.

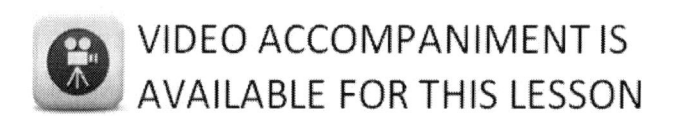

VIDEO ACCOMPANIMENT IS AVAILABLE FOR THIS LESSON

Head to http://learnguitar.nz

LESSON 4 – ARPEGGIO'S

Just a brief note on arpeggios after all the work we did on them last week.

With the arpeggio style of play, deep rich chords get the most benefit, as do flavour chords like the minor 7th's and add9's.

There are other benefits with arpeggio play, and the plectrum picking – the most obvious of which is that is allows up to play single note lines or licks from either within, or even outside of the chords that we are playing.

Working through a piece of music with licks in is no easy task, and will take practice. It will vary wildly depending on what you're playing, and this style of play is best reserved for a solo guitar lead-break or instrumental section of a song. It has to be carefully coordinated also, otherwise you can slip out of time quite easily.

Below is a hybrid of and old song from the sixties that is an example of combining lead lines with chord backing. I've also here a leadbreak to the song War, Bloody War, which is along the same lines, just more difficult.

Old Sixties Song Hybrid with Clean Picked Lead Lines

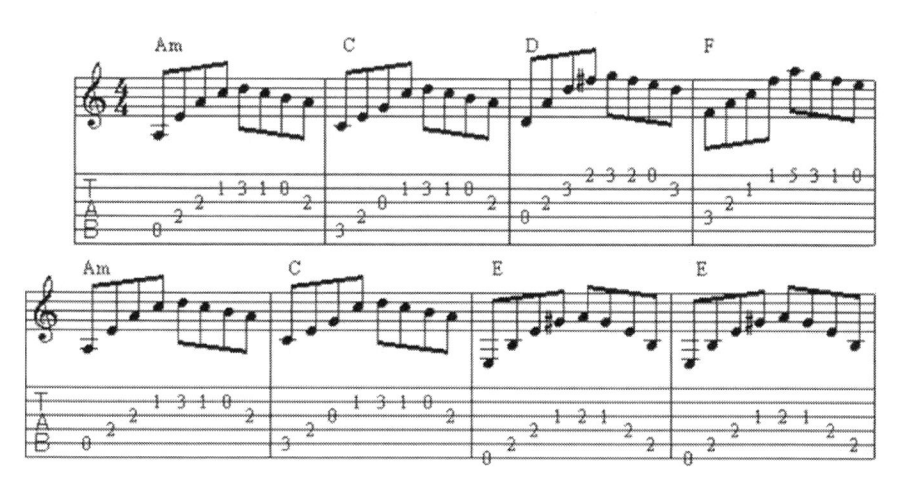

Here's the Lead Section for the song War, Bloody War.

Using the same chords as the chorus (G – D/F# - F – Em), the clean lead lines are really effective and providing a solo break on a single guitar. If you can play it accurately, it will sound as if there is a lot more going on than what there actually is.

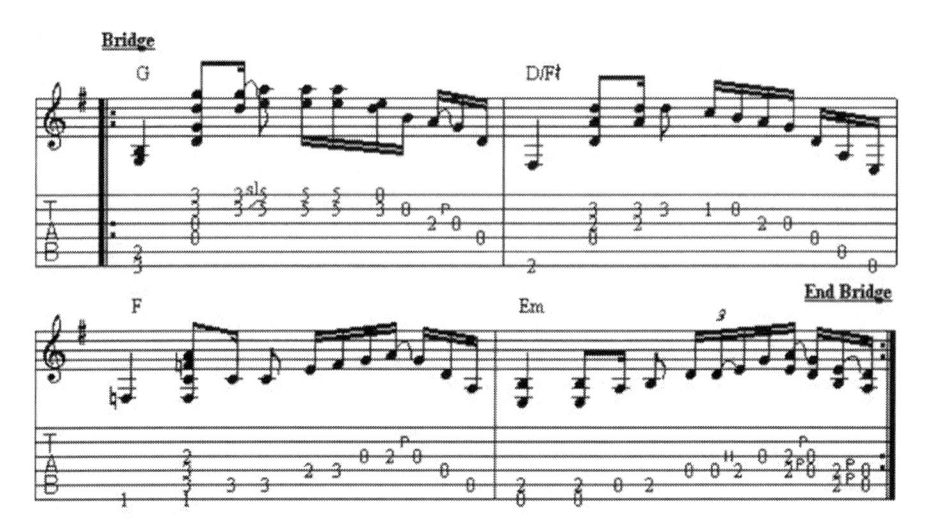

Good luck and good playing!

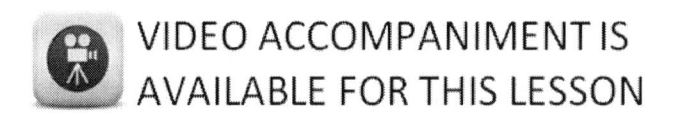

VIDEO ACCOMPANIMENT IS AVAILABLE FOR THIS LESSON

Head to http://learnguitar.nz

SESSION 5

What's in store this Session?

To begin with, we've another scale to learn. As always, these should be the core of our practice. The build strength and dexterity into our left hand, and work on the coordination between left and right – something which is often glanced over or passed quickly by – but is extremely important. So keep plugging away at your scales. Test yourself for the notes on the fretboard, start to learn them to heart.

For something exciting and off-the-beaten-track, there's a little jazz beauty that's transcribed in full. It's a wonderful piece of music, derived straight from some interesting flavour chords. It's tough and tricky for the left hand, with new chord shapes and will prove to be a real workout. Left hand techniques will remain relatively unchanged, although the arpeggio version has some challenging lead ideas which should keep you all working hard.

Further to the blues work already covered, we're going to start to add some lead licks to this as well. It's hard and its difficult, but it's well worth the practice, and then next week we'll be putting all our blues techniques together and making one giant great blues piece of music.

LESSON 1 – SCALE WORK

Here is the latest instalment of our scale work. It's in the seventh position, with the starting root note played by the 2nd finger on the eighth fret.

It is a relatively simple scale, with no stretches and no notes out of position.

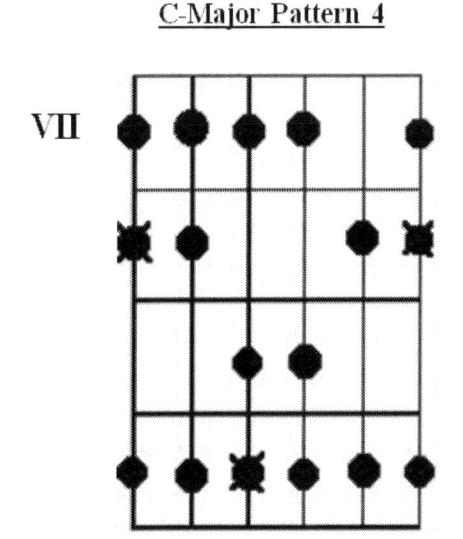

C-Major Pattern 4

VII

With your scales, you should start experimenting with different keys and different positions. Just like the Root Notes of our barre chords, with scales, by changing the root note you can change the scale. Still play the pattern the same, just literally alter the root note.

It's good practice as well to get used to using them in different positions. Even further, if you've got an electric guitar try and do patterns 1, 2 and 3 in the positions beyond the 12th fret. They are identical, just a little more squeezed for the fingers. Make sure you use the same fingerings, however.

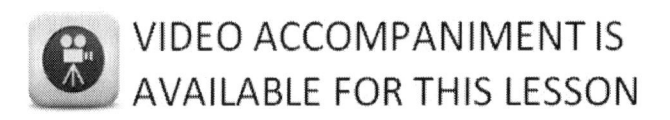

VIDEO ACCOMPANIMENT IS AVAILABLE FOR THIS LESSON

Head to http://learnguitar.nz

LESSON 2 – HOW ABOUT SOME JAZZ?

Jazz guitar is one of the most difficult styles of all to play on the guitar. It is also one of the loveliest.

Jazz guitarists have a knowledge of theory, scales, chords, fingerings and techniques which is quite unsurpassed by any other individual style. The ability to play very fast legato lines, match scales with chords through as much as a dozen key changes in one section, and most of all to keep that classic jazz-groove cruising along, is a tall order indeed, and very few musicians are up to the kind of discipline this requires.

However, without getting quite into the jazz boat, we can take a little of this and a little of that and come up with something as jazzy as the best the big bands could ever offer.

As practice, it's great to get the left hand away from standard fingerings and into something a little more complex and interesting. And with our right hand, we can apply all the great arpeggio ideas and fingerpicking techniques we've learned – and with the new chords, it'll sound like something out of this world.

First though, we must learn a few new chords.

Play the fretted notes only – i.e. no open strings (notes not played by a finger are muffled)

maj7

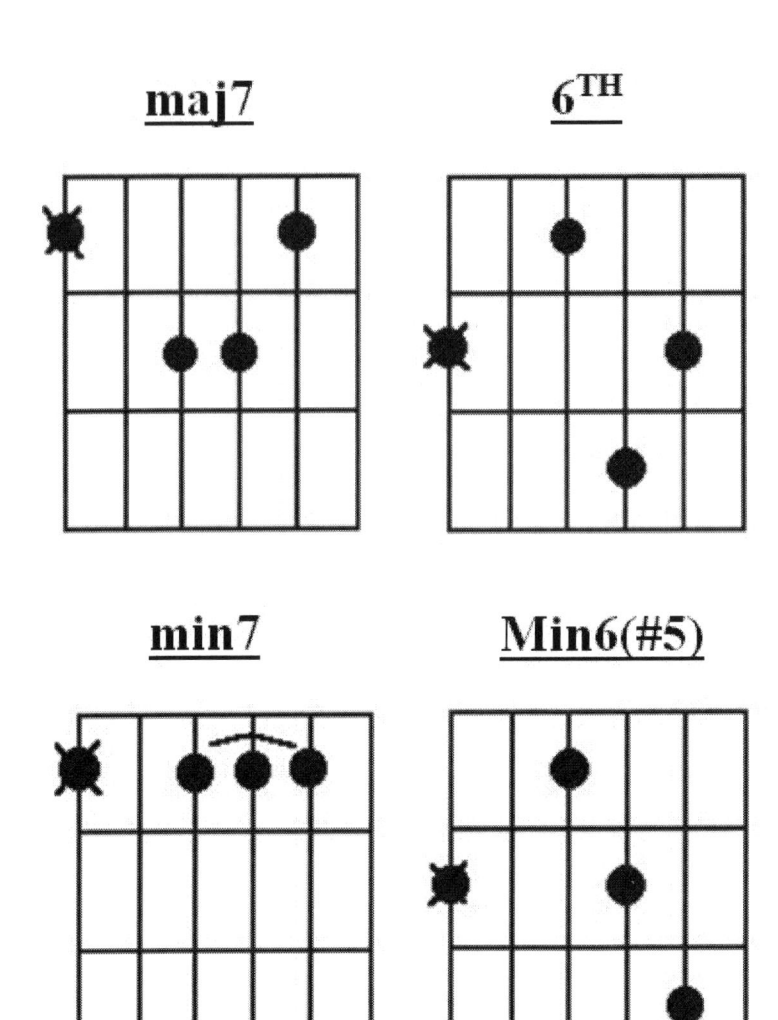

6TH

min7

Min6(#5)

7(addflat3)

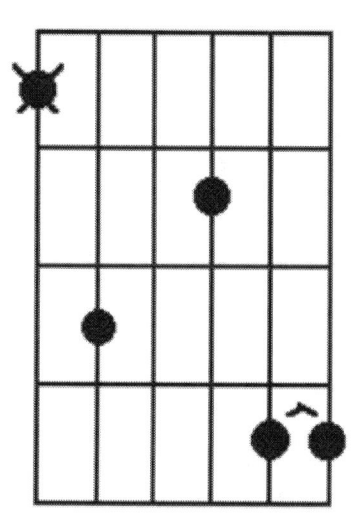

This is the Jazz Chord Progression in its most basic form. A lot of jazz standards and music is usually no more than what is below, and maybe a quick scrawl in the margin of the page to say what the feel is.

Jazz Standard

Gmaj7	G6	Gmaj7	G6
Gmaj7	G6	Gmaj7	G6
Bm7	Cmaj7	Bm7	Bbmin6(#5)
Bm7	Bbmin6(#5)	Am7	G#7(add flat3)
G#7(add flat3)			

Jazz Standard

Fingerpicked, with gentle swing style

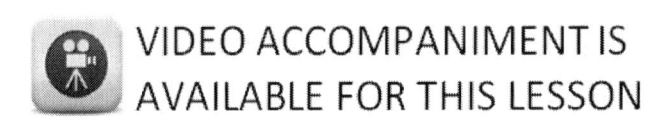

VIDEO ACCOMPANIMENT IS AVAILABLE FOR THIS LESSON

Head to http://learnguitar.nz

Jazz Standard

Arpeggio Style, fast with pick attack.

VIDEO ACCOMPANIMENT IS AVAILABLE FOR THIS LESSON

Head to http://learnguitar.nz

LESSON 3 – TRUE BLUES IN E

Up till now, we've been quite happily playing our blues. We've been strumming the twelve bar, we've been doing riff work, and for the brave, you may have even fingerpicked it a little bit.

We've learned about triplets, and how Blues and swing music is often scored into music and tablature. We know how to play a Pentatonic scale, which is the primary scale for any licks or lead work within the blues.

So what are we going to do – we're going to learn some more, and then we're going to put it all together.

What we have here is a whole lot of new techniques, all designed for solo guitar. Next week we're going to incorporate all our ideas, all our skills and all our techniques into one piece of music.

Remember also, that while it might be quite easy to pull off 12-bars of music in front of your mother or your friends, music is about songs, and songs are generally at least three minutes long. Say that's about 50 lots of twelve bars. So in effect, you have to play 600 bars. Now, the idea of learning all these techniques is so that you apply them into your playing. Remember you have 600 bars to play, so if you put them all into the first 24 bar introduction, then you're going to sound pretty boring by the time bar 100 rolls around, let alone 600! So you apply them in where they are meant to be applied. Don't try to do a crazy triplet lick while the singer in saying his part. Don't switch from a Riff-based shuffle to the open-chord version in the middle of the drummer's crash and bash solo section. Save it up and try to build things a little. Start off subtle – throw the fancy stuff in later. With the piece of music further up, as much as possible has been crammed into 36 bars, but that's not the way you would play it. You would play each technique at a different point. Got it?

Good! Well then, let's learn something new!

Starting to use our Pentatonic scale for the blues.

We all know the Em Pentatonic scale. We can go up and down, we get the fingerings right, we know the scale.

But what about how to use it?

Here's some licks to start it all rolling.

Licks.

Let's take our Pentatonic scale, our knowledge of triplets, and our Hammer-on's and combine them to make something interesting.

Here's a few examples. Make sure you get the fluidity of them correct so they are smooth.

Below is an example of a triplet lick, using a Hammer on. The notes are from the Em pentatonic scale. Take very careful not of the timing. When you have the hang of it, try to do a whole bar, and per the second half.

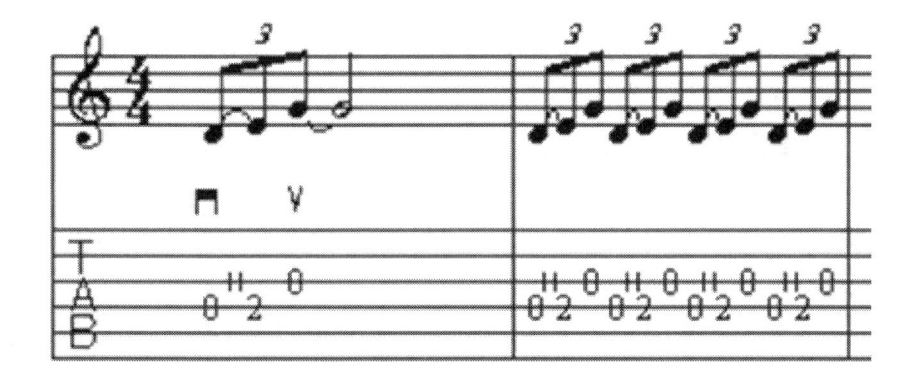

Below is exactly the same lick again, just using the 3rd and 2nd string notes from the Em Pentatonic scale instead of the 4th and 3rd as above. Again, get the hang of it first. When you do the bar, get it smooth and silky.

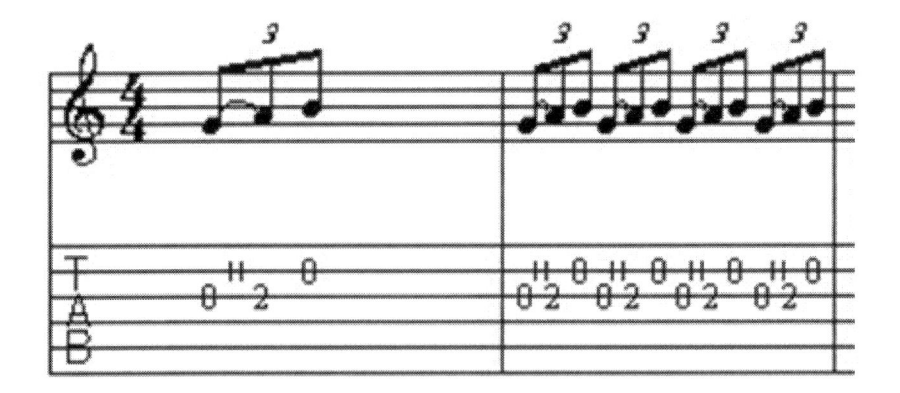

Below are two more of the same licks, on the 5th and 4th strings, and then the 2nd and 1st strings. Remember to up an up/down motion with the right hand for all these licks as per in the first example.

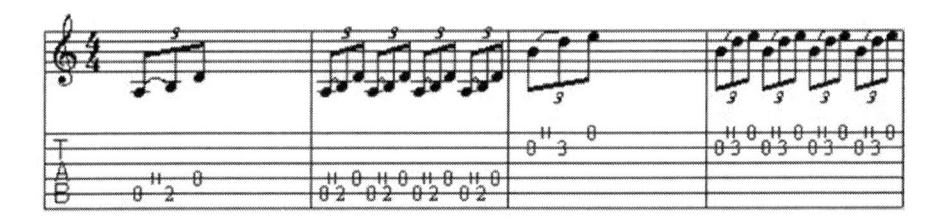

Okay, so what say we take each of the licks above and put them all together for one giant lick. Well not so giant really, just one bar, but by using all four of the two-string combinations as on the previous page, we get a lick that goes through just about the entire pentatonic scale. Real good fun. Have a go. Remember that you have to get it smooth and flowing, with each group of three even in length.

What about triplet licks that are like our shuffle, and have the longer note first with a quick note before starting over. Have a look at the lick below; the timing for it just follows the rhythm, as opposed to jumping into the **123 123 123 123** of triplets. The timing is more of a **1 &2 &3 &4 &**

Here is another lick using the same timing. This one throws in another new technique – a quick slide up to the 5th fret, second string. Now that note is not strictly in the scale pattern that we are playing, but as we all know, the 5th fret, 2nd string note is the same as the open 1st string note, which is in our scale pattern. So we can use it. Same with the 4th fret 3rd string note. Have a go, it's a great lick.

```
                    3
  ┌─────────────────────────────────────────┐
  │         ╭─╮                       ♪─♪   │
  │    ♪    ♪  ♪   ╭─╮   ♪─♪              │
  │                ♪  ♪                    │
  │         3        3                     │
  └─────────────────────────────────────────┘
  ┌─────────────────────────────────────────┐
  │   sl                                    │
  T──╱─5────────3──────────3────────────────
  A─────────────────4─────────4────2───0────
  B─────────────────────────────────────────
```

Okay, so the licks on the previous page are pure LEAD licks, being based in a scale and picking single notes.

The following licks are what we call Rhythm Based Licks, being lead type licks taken directly from the chords that we are playing. The below licks have come from our open chord shuffle that we learned in the beginners course. All we're doing is taking a part rhythm section, a couple of pull-off's, a bit of right hand picking (note the up/down motion of the right hand – nothing actually changes other than instead of strumming, we pick) and combine it all together into a very effective lick. These are well worth the practice, as if you get them good, at a fast pace, they sound absolutely marvellous.

Here's one based on the E chord.

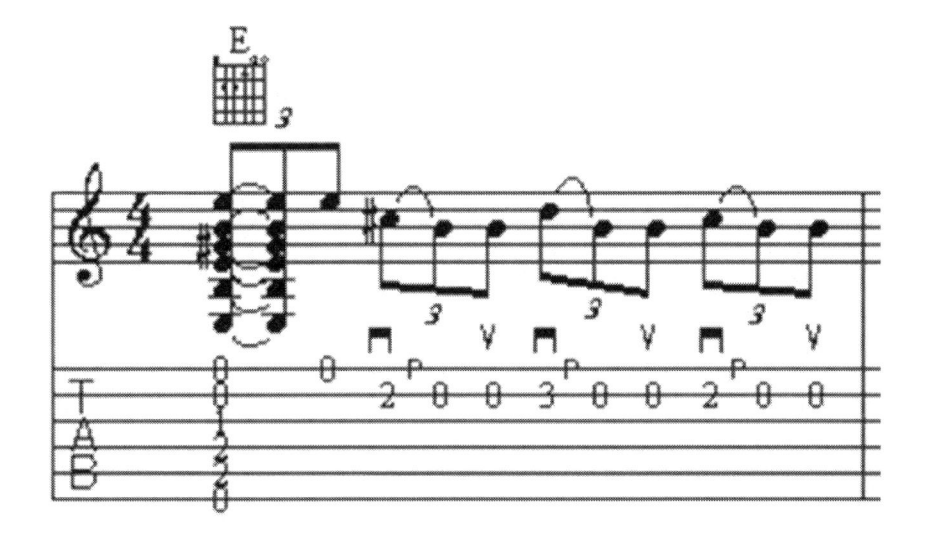

And here's one based on the A7 chord.

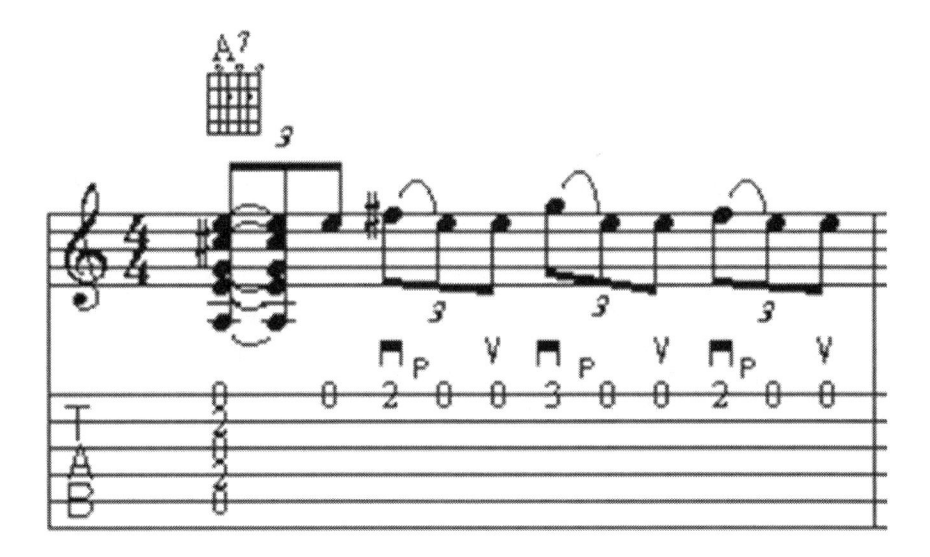

Make sure to practice these licks well – when applied into a blues piece of music (or anything else too!) their effect is instant, and can really lift the piece up.

Have fun. Good luck and good playing!

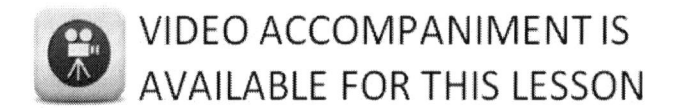

VIDEO ACCOMPANIMENT IS AVAILABLE FOR THIS LESSON

Head to http://learnguitar.nz

SESSION 6

Okay, by now you should have a good grasp of all the various techniques and ideas that have been put forward. What we're going to be doing in this session and then in 7 & 8 is consolidating all these ideas and techniques into a variety of songs and pieces of music. Naturally, with any songs of your own that you have written, or any covers that you have learned, you can use any or all of these techniques. You could even try a few of your own.

What you will not be doing however, is playing boring old strum-and-chords guitar any longer. Any piece can be improved on with the guitar by applying a bit of thought and a bit of technique, and it is then that the guitar really begins to sound like the beautiful instrument that it is.

This session is a little different again, in what you will be learning. There is, of course, the customary scale pattern to be learned. This will bring the total number of scales patterns you know to five, and once again, in cannot be stressed how important these are for practice. They also make a great warmup before any practice session, and regardless of the exercise, they get your hands all limbered and ready for the difficult pieces you are no doubt working on.

We have the second instalment in songwriting, which covers another approach to the theory behind killer hooks and catchy choruses and verses. Once again, no one can ever teach you how to write that hit song, but there are some certain rules which, when applied, can make your life a little easier when working on melody or song.

The third part of this session is a Blues piece. It's a great piece of music, and incorporates all the techniques we've learned to date into one piece. Work on getting it exact. It'll repay you by sounding really good if you do.

LESSON 1 – C-MAJOR SCALE PATTERN 5

The next of our Scale patterns, this one has a couple of things of note to be careful of.

This pattern is in the 9th position, being 1 finger per fret starting from the 9th fret. The lowest note of the scale is however, on the 8th fret, so just like we did in Pattern 2, we have to pull our first finger back to make these notes on the 6th and 5th strings. Remember to be careful not to move your hand though, only the finger.

Of second point to note, when the scale moves to the 2nd and 1st strings, it does change position. Your hand must move from the 9th position to the 10th. Remember to move back from the 10th position to the 9th position when descending the scale.

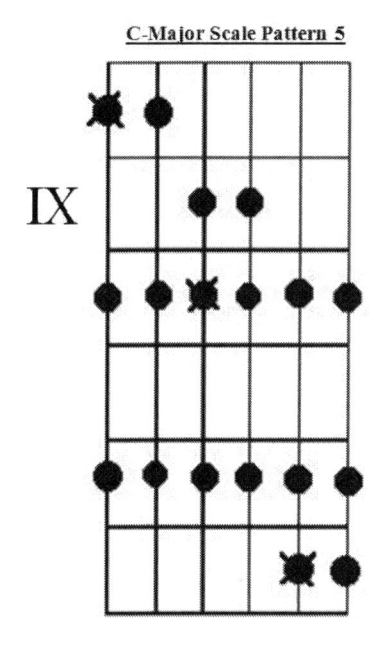

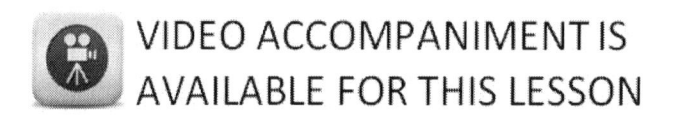

C-Major Scale Pattern 5

IX

VIDEO ACCOMPANIMENT IS AVAILABLE FOR THIS LESSON

Head to http://learnguitar.nz

LESSON 2 – SONGWRITING

Songwriting is an art. But like any art, anybody can learn it. Also like any art, the more you do it, the better you become.

Some musicians have troves of songs. Hundreds, thousands. The composer Schumann wrote over 600 published pieces – I hate to imagine how many more he wrote and confined to the rubbish bin!

So write, write and write again. Take a song you know and change the chords to go backwards. That's good enough to be new song. Now file the sound away in your memory banks and do it again. Change the key. Change the tempo (speed). Try it fingerpicked. Play it strummed or with arpeggio's. Or combinations. And that's all with some chords that you've borrowed from an existing song. Change one chord. Sound any different. Try another. Now you're writing! Change it back. Try it again and again. Keep filing the sounds into your mind. Soon, you might have a hot verse and chorus and just as you're looking for that cool intro, you'll go back to this sound that you were mucking around with a few days ago. Presto – you've got the hook!

Songwriting is an art, and just like any art, it needs to be practiced.

You're guitar playing is an art, but where the guitar is the canvas and your fingers the brushes, songwriting is an art where the song's structure and melodies are the canvas, and your guitar the brush. And, of course, how you hold your brush will affect how you write your songs.

Some players play fast lead lines and supercharged riffs. They play with technical skill. Their skills sometimes sell more records than their songs, but it's one way to play.

Some players play extremely simply. Bob Dylan knows only a few chords, yet his record sales are tremendous. His writing is prolific too, with hundreds of songs penned from him, most of them poetry made to fit around those few chords.

Some players have a technique they favour most. They might write all their songs fingerpicked. They design the songs and the chords to get the most from fingerpicking. Same with some heavy rock bands. The styles of playing are naturally related, but so far away from each other on the spectrum that the common comparisons are few and far between. And the songs – both types work of course and have their audience, but again common comparisons are as plentiful as eighty-year old ladies at MegaDeth concerts.

Some players, like Finger of Fire Guitar School students, can fingerpick as easily as the can strum as easy as they can arpeggiate.

So we can write and write and write. We can use our knowledge of theory and structure to write precise, well designed music. We can play a single chord a dozen different ways with two dozen different sounds. What we cannot teach, that nobody can, is how to get that initial spark. Only by spending time on the guitar will you get that.

Now we've always organised our guitar time around practice-type playing. Where we sit down and practice an exercise and a piece a dozen times, before moving on and doing the same with the next. Most of us have busy lives – we never get to spend as much time on the guitar as we'd like. But now we're going to relax things a little bit. Of course, you've still got to do the exercise otherwise you'll never get the techniques! But just as importantly, we've got to spend some time enjoying our instrument. We've have to play to bring a smile to our faces, to lift our heart after a heavy day, to watch our wives and husbands, our children and our friends, to see the joy that music can bring to them – to be the one bringing it to them!

So try to relax and play. Toy with chords. Toy with techniques. The pressure of learning and aspiring to be a better guitarist is always going to be there, even after 20 years, but now we should sit back and enjoy a little of the fruits of our labours.

And I mean ENJOY! No stress, no funny, fuddy duddy chord changing problems here. No upset spats about a riff that just won't work. That's for later in the day when we get serious about this practice again. Relaxing is for now. Enjoying.

And you know what?

When you start to enjoy, that's when that classic hook will come!

So you have to divide songwriting away from playing. You playing is just the tool that we use to write songs with. Songwriting is an art that demands a comfortable state of mind. You can't write songs to demand. You can't write songs by demand. I would never sign a three record contract when I know perfectly well that I've only enough material for two!

Songrwriting is an art – and as such it cannot be turned on and off by demand. Writing under financial pressure or incentive could very well be the type of writing that turns the tap off!

Which brings us to formula writing.

Notice how some bands sometimes release a new album that sounds just like the last with new lyrics, a couple of rearranged riffs, and a few new lead licks to keep the techo's happy?

In the late 1980's there was a whole rash of this Power Ballad thing. You needed a golden singer, rocky guitars, heaps of makeup, rich chords fingerpicked or arpeggio'd, a heavy part in the middle with power chords over acoustic guitars, enough reverb to sound like they're jamming in the Grand Canyon, a quick guitar solo then a slow fade over multiple choruses at the end. That was your Power Ballad.

Power Ballad's are a formula. Quite a complex one, and one that certainly takes a bit of talent to pull off, but nonetheless, a formula. Do it more than twice in your career and you'll hit a brick wall. But hey, for your three record contract, you managed to fill the albums, right? Sure, but you sure as hell won't be re-signed or signed to another label. The bored public will see to that.

A simpler type of formula writing is doing 12-Bar Blues the entire time. Sure play blues and play hell out of 12-Bar Blues, but play with the variations, take the standards and add your own personality. The standard we've always worked on, the one we'll continue to work on is only one of thousands. Use them all, butcher them all, do it YOUR way. YOUR WAY!

Any song that exclusively uses the I IV V variations could be called formula. But there are millions... billions of songs with I IV V. The difference is the indefinite number of ways to do it (the same could be said for the blues too, but blues has a great tendency to be approximately within a few tempo's and due to its blues rhythm doesn't allow much flexibility sometimes). With I IV V you can stop. You can start. You can pause. You can breathe. You can speed up, slow down, double time, triple time and half-time. Your lyrics can scream and shout, they can whisper or hiss. They can be melodic or they can yell. I IV V is a formula, but it's a good one!

Formula's can and do work, but there is always going to be this need for your own stamp, your individuality. Without it, then there is a formula. And even if you do have a stamp and a couple of great hooks. Don't use them in every song. You need multiple stamps. Multiple hooks. Multiple personalities? Ha, no!

But you need to approach every song as a new canvas, same guitar brush. Perhaps some new colours you picked up on the way from your last canvas. And the only way you'll get this is by relaxing, enjoying, and having a good time. Songwriting is not about pressure either, and be careful not to get stressed that you've been playing the guitar for six hours all through a Saturday afternoon and still haven't written anything. Let it come. It will, and when it does, it'll be great.

Play, enjoy, be creative. Take the standards and create your own. Have fun!

LESSON 3 – THE CIRCLE OF FIFTHS

The Circle of Fifths is a tool that Classically trained musicians use to discover how many Sharps or Flats a particular key has.

This is very useful to guitarists also, but is of more relevance to theory purists. For the purposes of modern guitar and songwriting, it has applications also, but for the sharps and flats side, that is more of a reference.

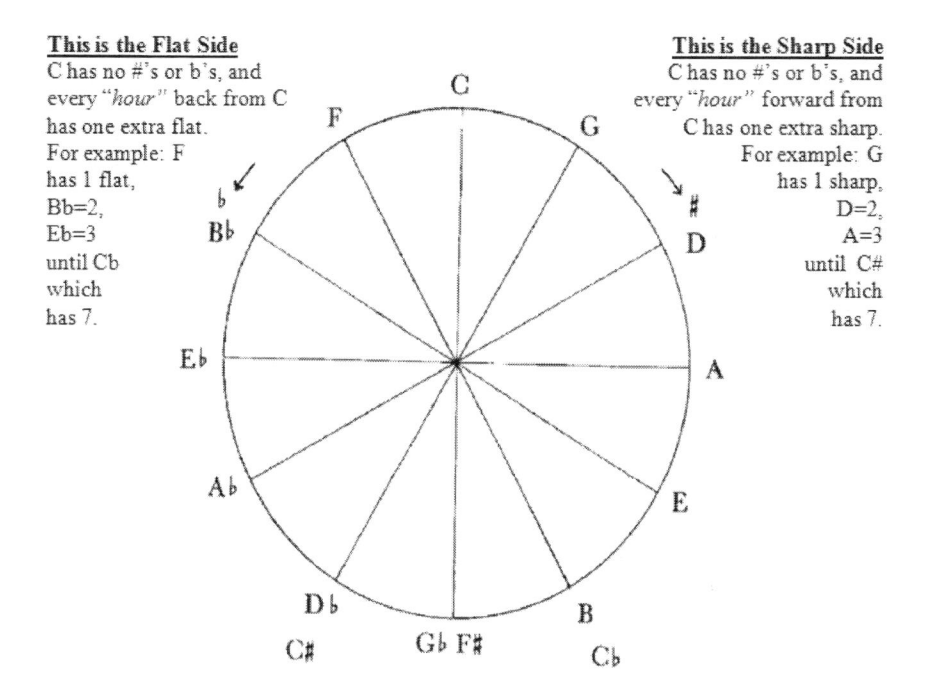

This is the Flat Side
C has no #'s or b's, and every *"hour"* back from C has one extra flat.
For example: F has 1 flat,
Bb=2,
Eb=3
until Cb
which
has 7.

This is the Sharp Side
C has no #'s or b's, and every *"hour"* forward from C has one extra sharp.
For example: G has 1 sharp,
D=2,
A=3
until C#
which
has 7.

Circle positions: C (top), G, D, A, E, B, Cb, Gb F#, Db, C#, Ab, Eb, Bb, F

It is very handy to modern songwriters for its potential to be used for interesting a unusual chord changes.

Modern songwriters generally begin with a Chord Progression, much like the ones that have been taught as examples for learning chords and testing yourself. Modern Musician's and guitarists generally begin with a chord prgression as such and then develop it. But how to get that original chord progression to begin with?

One way is to use our theory of knowing what chords for what keys, and that's a great way, including, of course, that although you have your theory, the only real rule is that if it sounds good, it is good! However, the Circle of Fifths can be used to find that elusive sound or that elusive chord that you're looking for.

To use it, pick a Key. We'll use C because it's right on 12 o'clock. Now immediately to the left you have C's 4th, or the Sub-Dominant. To the right you have C's 5th, or Dominant. That's our main chords for C. Good stuff so far. Okay, now when searching for that extra chord, why not go two clicks back from C, or two forward? They fit in nicely, and don't clash, but have a different sound. Try three clicks, or four. They all work for the most part, and suddenly, we've got some great new sound coming through. Even though some may clash depending on what you're trying to say with your song, they certainly do add a great new sound to some pieces.

Musicians and songwriters like Billy Joel, Elton John and Paul Simon often used the circle of fifths in their music.

Here are some chord progressions quickly put together and the Circle of Fifths for reference again below.

Chord Progression No. 1

| C | | Bb F | | C | | Bb G | |

Chord Progression No. 2

| C | | Bb | | Eb | | F G | |

They're just a couple of quick ideas, but you start to get the idea of the potential of this.

As a finish to this songwriting lesson, here's one further note to do with 5ths.

When writing a phrase, and you want to go back to the Root Chord, the best way to go back is from the 5th. For example, in both progressions above, the last chord is G, which is the 5th of C. This is what leads back to the C chord best.

Not always the rule, but certainly true in a lot of cases. Naturally, your writing your own songs and it is your song, so you can do whatever you like!

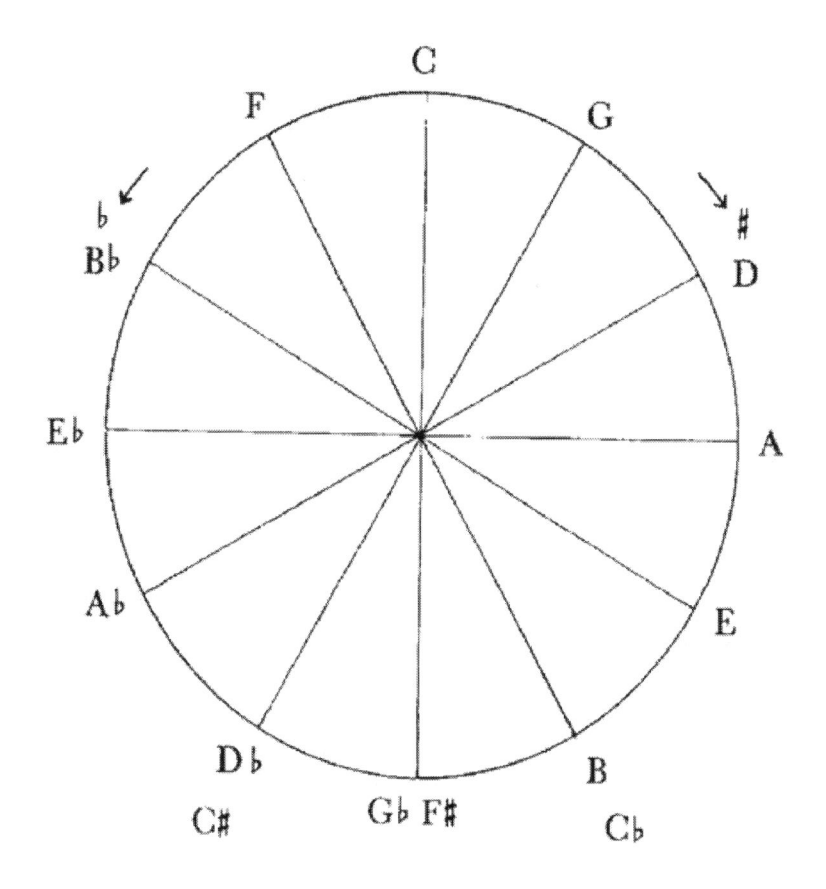

VIDEO ACCOMPANIMENT IS AVAILABLE FOR THIS LESSON

Head to http://learnguitar.nz

LESSON 4 - BLUES FOR SAM (12 BAR BLUES)

The following is a rendition of the blues using all the techniques, ideas, and other bits and pieces that we have learned. Spend a while going through it slowly. There's a couple of lead type licks that haven't been done yet, but are just natural extensions of what we've already learned.

Have a good time with it.

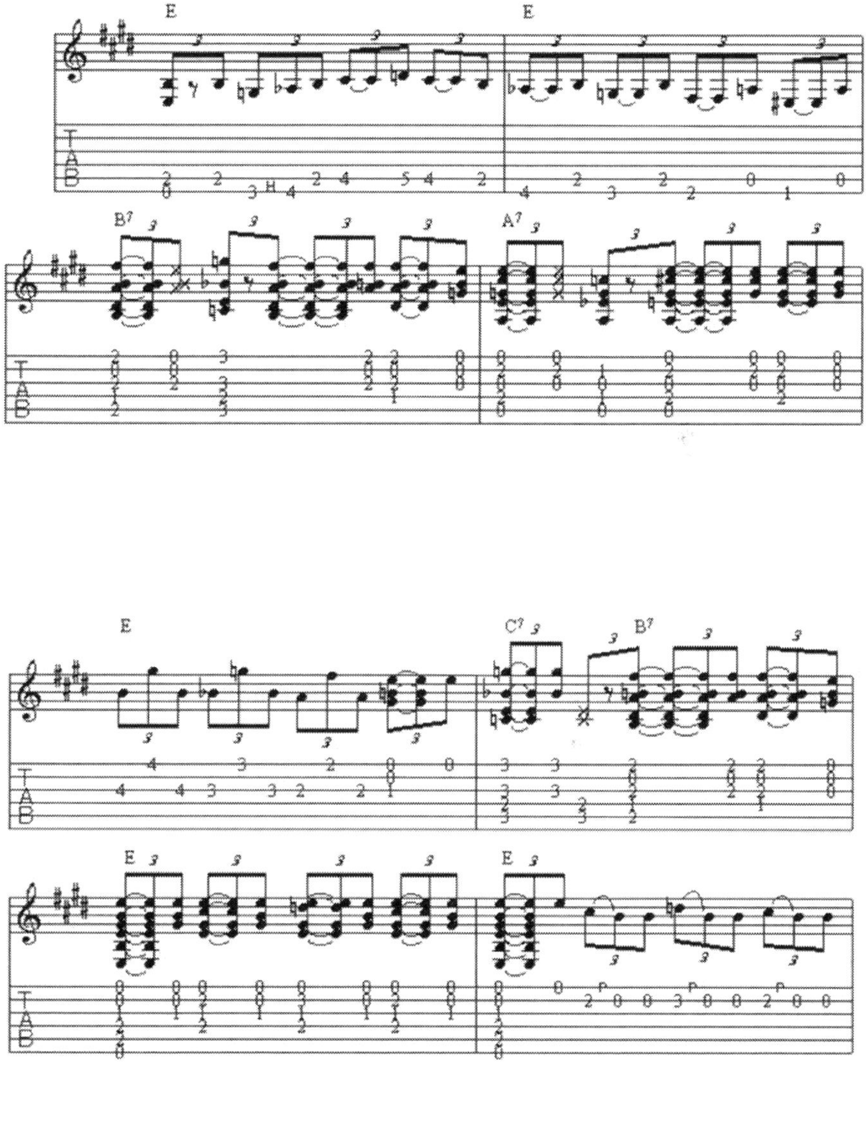
E
E
B7
A7
E
C7
B7
E
E

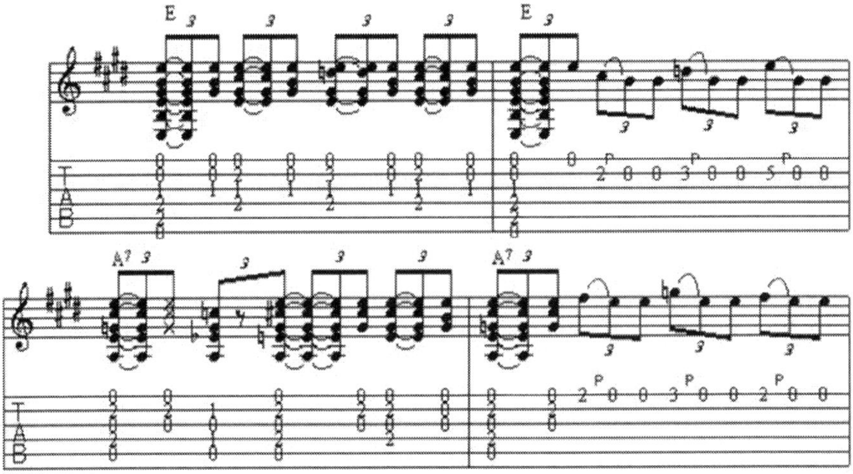
E
E
A7
A7

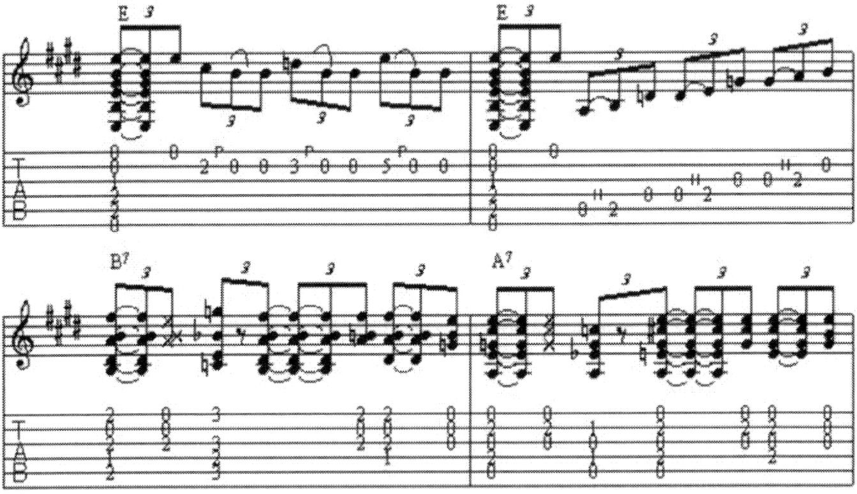
E
E
B7
A7

0

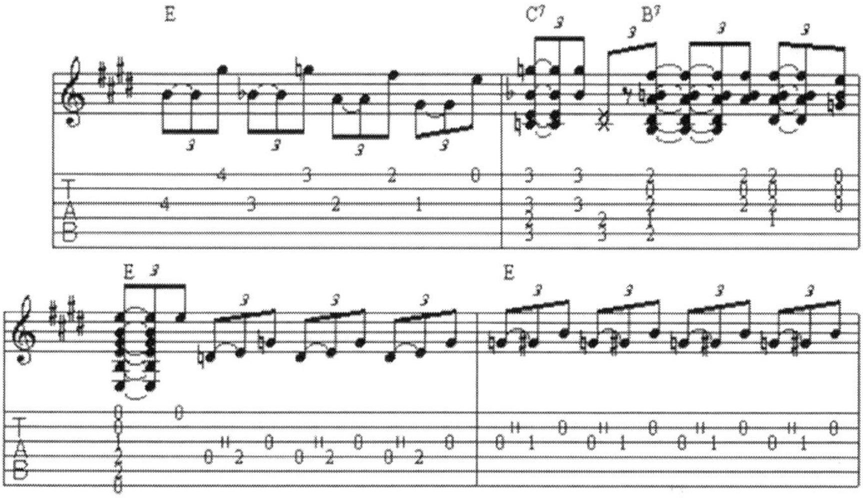

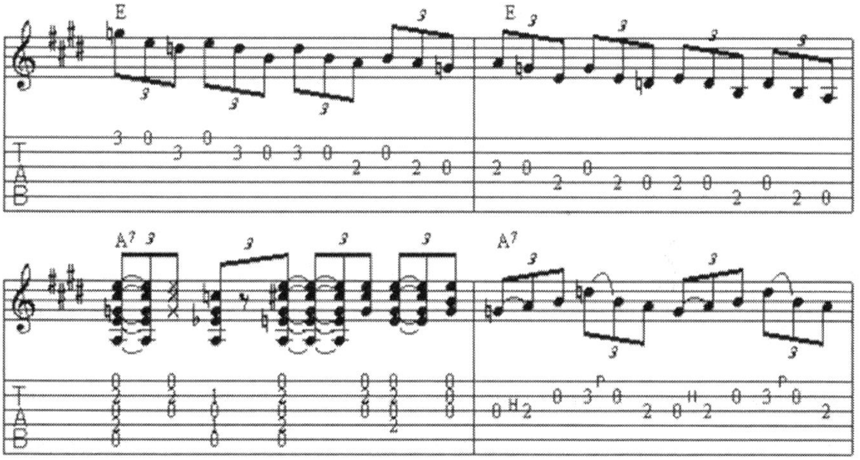

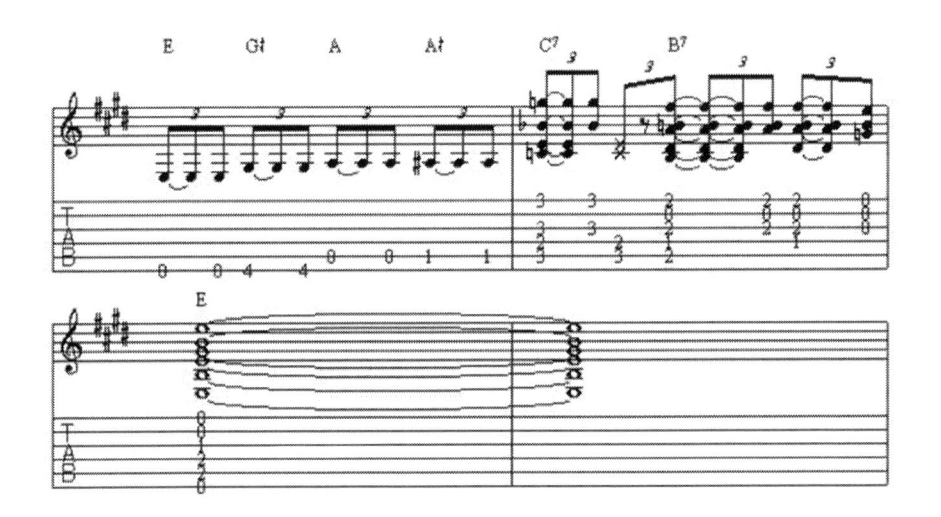

Good luck and Good Playing!

VIDEO ACCOMPANIMENT IS AVAILABLE FOR THIS LESSON

Head to http://learnguitar.nz

SESSION 7

Right then.

I hope all you guitar playing is going well. It certainly is a great instrument to play; good fun, challenging, exciting to listen to, immensely varied in style and sound. Yes, the guitar is a beautiful instrument.

But you still need pieces to play, songs and instrumentals. The purpose of Session's Seven and Eight is to start your "repertoire" building up. Session Seven here, is concerned with Instrumentals. There are two great pieces here for you to learn and play.

One is offbeat, with an unusual rhythm that'll keep you trying until you just sort of click into it. It's fingerpicked, but not any sort of standard pattern way we've learned yet. Sounds great and highly effective.

The other is more standard in its timing, just a little faster, and will really benefit from Right Hand technique, accents, and a sharp picking attack in certain sections, while a softer approach in others will sound best.

In addition to these two pieces, you have the other pieces from within in the course.

The blues is a real classy piece of music, and with its lead lines and slick triplet timing, if you've committed it to memory, it'll sound real sharp.

The Jazz piece we learned in Session 5 has a stunning sound I'm sure you know when cruising along with no gaps in the chord changing. Keep working at it.

Of course, you should also be building your own repertoire, whether it's from the fabulous amount of songs you've written, or be it just picking up on everything you hear. Buying music or downloading from the net is great too. Build your repertoire, keep adding whenever you can. It does wonders.

LESSON 1 - A QUICK FORAY

This is a ditty little arpeggiated piece that really benefits from full control of your right hand.

Play it quite fast, and put real emphasis into the strumming of the chords.

Where it is employing the "descending bass line" through the Cadd9, G/B, A7sus4 and G chords, play this with a kind of subtle approach, and accenting the part where the G chord has the multiple strums with the different timing.

With the Chorus type part, notice the arpeggio difference in the C chord to the D/F# and G. Try and make this come through with an accent on the C and it will lift the chorus right up.

Allow all the strings to continue ringing as well, and this will make the sound richer and fuller.

It is an example of how simple and standard chords can be made to sound a whole lot different just from a bit of unusual timing (nothing like Hou Day X 7 though!) and a lot of concentration on what the right hand is doing.

Also as one other technique to learn we have what is called a GLISS. This is when you pick the notes of a chord a lot faster than an arpeggio, but still far slower than an actual strum. It's quite a tricky technique and is quite hard to represent on paper. The best way to do it is probably to write it as it has been, with the 32nd notes representing the first half beat of the bar. Not quite prefect, but if you try the technique you'll see how it works.

Have fun.

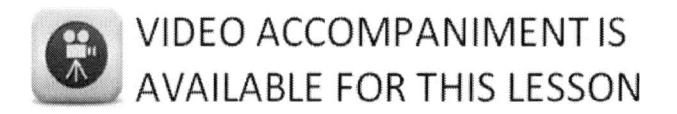

VIDEO ACCOMPANIMENT IS AVAILABLE FOR THIS LESSON

Head to http://learnguitar.nz

A Quick Foray

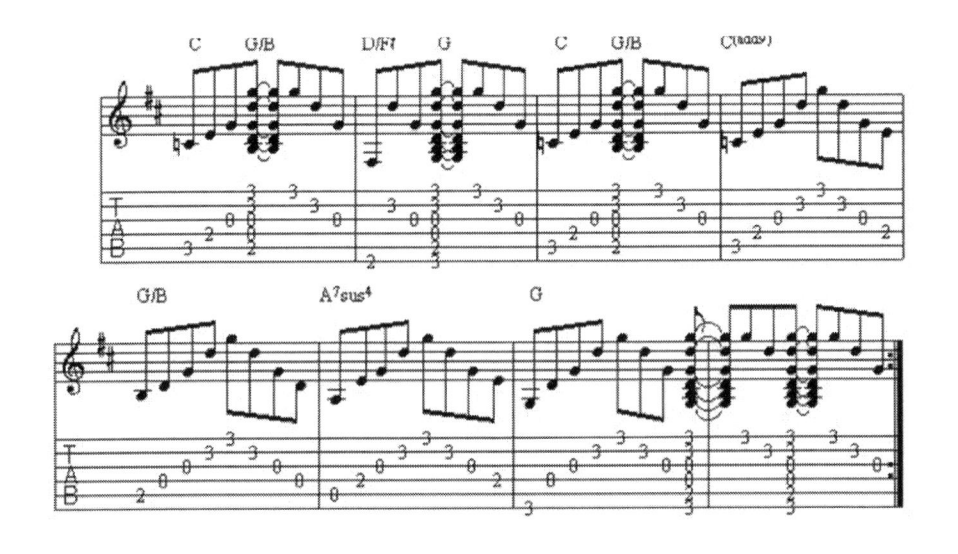

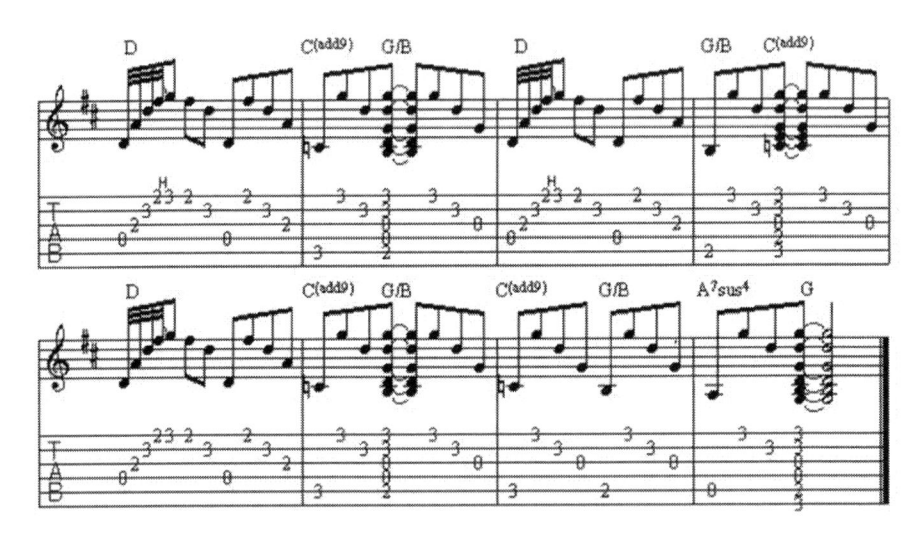

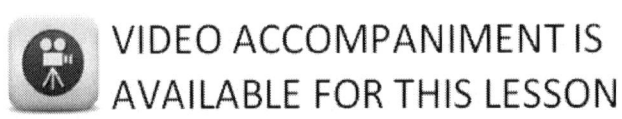

VIDEO ACCOMPANIMENT IS AVAILABLE FOR THIS LESSON

Head to http://learnguitar.nz

LESSON 2 - HOU DAY X 7

Yep, that's the name of this piece! There's no point even trying to explain where the name came from – it could just be one of those unusual musician things!

Anyway, this piece is a little different in that is almost entirely OFFBEAT. It has a bass line that does most of the work in the song, while the treble (higher) parts of each chord are played consistently on the "&" part of the beat. So in effect, the bass line here is holding down the rhythm while the treble is playing a melody, which is happening away from the bass, and on the off part off the beat – hence, offbeat.

The timing is quite tricky to get the hang of, but once you seem to have it, keep the same going throughout and it sounds really good. This one deserves some work, so go hard at it.

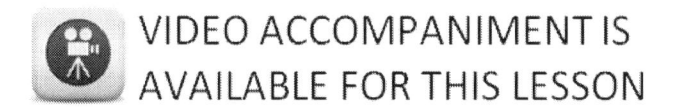

VIDEO ACCOMPANIMENT IS AVAILABLE FOR THIS LESSON

Head to http://learnguitar.nz

HOU DAY X 7

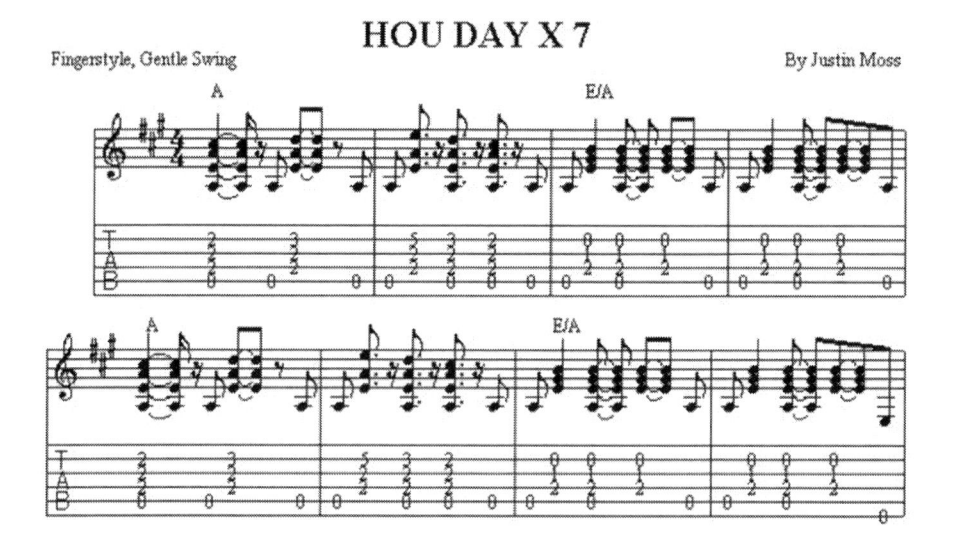

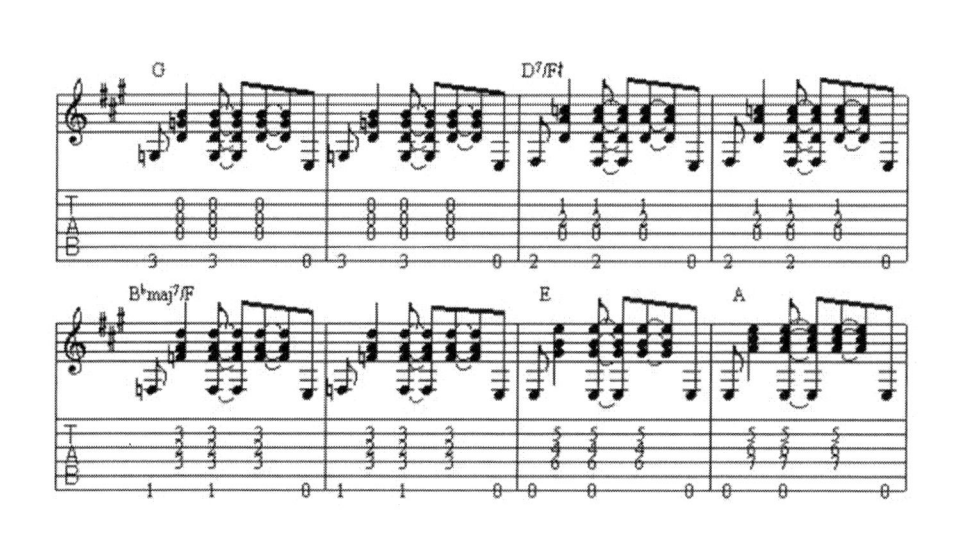

Fingerstyle, Gentle Swing

By Justin Moss

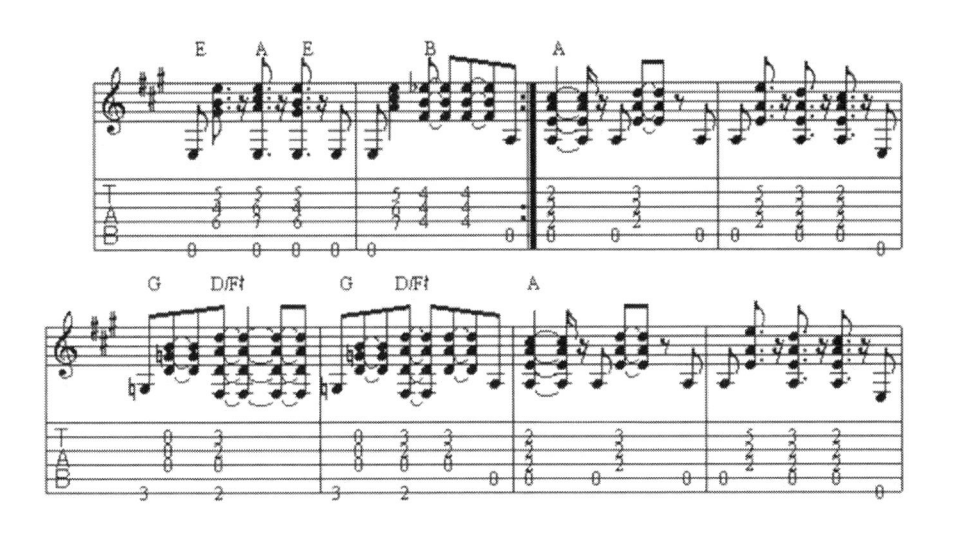

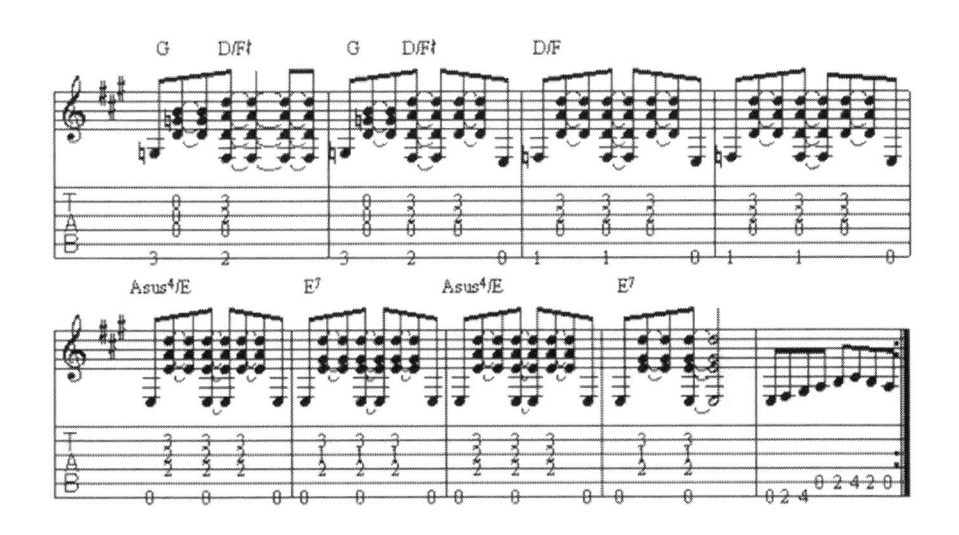

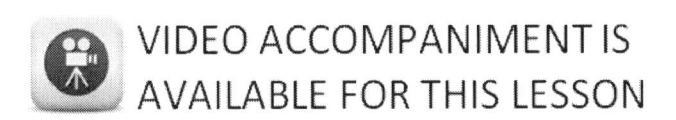

VIDEO ACCOMPANIMENT IS AVAILABLE FOR THIS LESSON

Head to http://learnguitar.nz

SESSION 8

Okay, we've reached the end, the pinnacle of the Fingers of Fire Guitar School Intermediate Course.

By now, your scales should be providing exercise, your techniques should be building nicely to the point where they are smooth and are very prevalent in the pieces you are playing. In fact, to couple these, your "repertoire" should be building also.

In addition to the pieces you've learned throughout the course, you should be adding your own pieces, whether they be ones you've written yourself, or picked up from other musicians, the radio, CD's or the Internet. Either way, you should be building a real database of great music to play, to impress yourself and others.

One thing we've always done so far is to play instrumental music. One of the pieces here in this session is a song with vocals.

I'm sure you'll enjoy these pieces, and I'm sure you've enjoyed the course also. I hope you have learned a lot about how songs work, about how guitar playing works to make songs.

Keep practicing and keep learning.

LESSON 1 - TRUEST KIND

This is a beautiful, lilting ballad written in the key of D, and using all the chords of the key, as well as a few Accidentals in there as well, usually for the purposes of keeping the Bass runs going through nice and smoothly.

The chords work together like an absolute dream, and are a testament to Diatonic Writing. Check out the chords using your theory, and have a good look at the structure as well.

It's not too difficult to play, and the chords are quite straightforward, being straight from the contents of the course so far.

Take note also how the song uses increases and decreases of speed and well as dynamics in volume to suggest the different sections.One other technique is Right Hand ATTACK, where not only do the picking fingers try to pick louder or softer, they use a sort of INTENSITY when picking the strings at certain points. This is known as ATTACK, and when playing a solo acoustic guitar, really adds atmosphere and interest to the piece without going over-the-top. The song manages to take the listener into an enjoyment of the music without presenting it in an in-your-face type of situation.

Play it well and play it properly and smoothly. After you've got the music playing well and smoothly, start to add the lyrics.

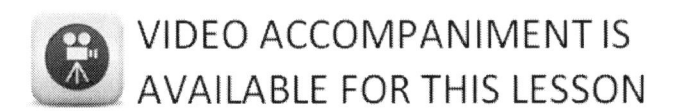

VIDEO ACCOMPANIMENT IS AVAILABLE FOR THIS LESSON

Head to http://learnguitar.nz

Truest Kind

Fingerstyle, gently, allow to ring

By Justin Moss

E
I love you ....
I love you ....
D/F#
G
E/G#
A
G
E/G#
A
He turns to her ...... I Love you too..............
I Love you too
D
A/C#
Bm
A6
Once in a million.... years....
You meet a couple like this...
and, once in a life - time....
You see a love like this...

A6/G♯
F♯m
she says to, him ....
E
I love you ....
I love you ....
D/F♯
G
E/G♯
A
He turns to her ...... I Love you too..............
I Love you too
'cause it's

True Love... of the Truest Kind..... True Love the kind you find.......

True Love... of the Truest......... Kind.................

Once in a million years....... You see a love like this...

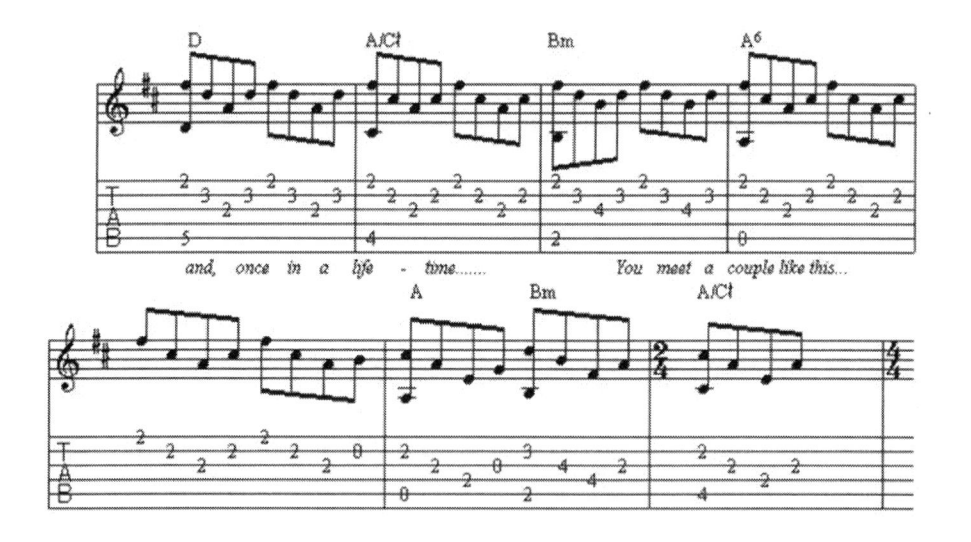

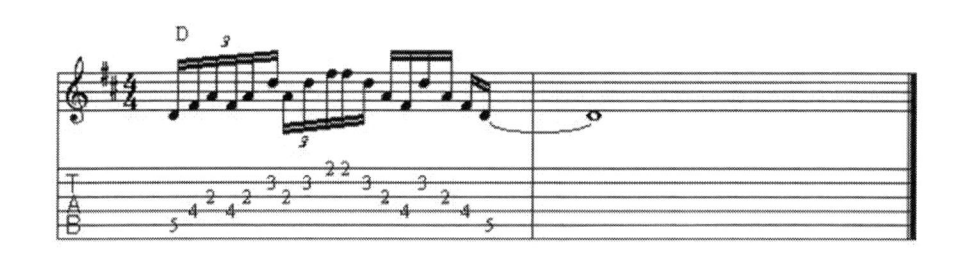

and, once in a life - time....... You meet a couple like this...

VIDEO ACCOMPANIMENT IS AVAILABLE FOR THIS LESSON

Head to http://learnguitar.nz

LESSON 2 - THE OLD BALLAD SONG

This is another one of those songs that has a real delicious melody with which the guitar can be such a complement to. The chords are lovely, being a I IV V base progression, with the II (minor) thrown in for a bit of flavour.

Notice that the II (minor) is only one note in difference to the IV (Major) as well, which in a song like this divided into the two four bar phrases, ending once on II and next on IV, the difference between the two chords isn't that great. As such, the song comes across as being quite subtle with its changes, with from a guitarist's point of view, being able to play the same licks on either chord, and still getting a different feel.

The arrangement here is one which works equally well for Solo Guitar and performance, as much as for the same style in a Band Setting. The only aspect which could be expanded on in a band situation would be the lead break, which could be a lot more conventional with Bass and Drums to fill in all the gaps. The rest of the structure could apply easily.

In fact to go a step further, this arrangement has been approached almost as if it were a pure instrumental, and only backing off to give the vocalist/lyrics room. The first 8 bars are stating the theme with good sweeping arpeggio's and gliss's, then when the verse begins the guitar backs off to strumming the chords only, with a couple of very subtle licks after the singing stops. As a lead up to the chorus, the final C chord of the verse is an arpeggiate'd descending bass lick which works really well. To get the maximum effect, strike quite hard with the pick and really accent this part.

For the solo section, it is important to not lose track of what the beat is doing. When trying to give a solo performance over set chords in a piece such as this, we don't really want to just end up repeating all the things we did over the verse and choruses, so instead must resort to some single string picking in the G Pentatonic Major Scale and G Major Scale. While this is easy over a full backing, it's a bit more difficult on your own, and I'm sure that you'll be able to develop what's here even further. (Note that for the G major Pentatonic scale, Em is the relative minor of G major, so the Em Penta contains exactly the same notes then G major, just with a changed root note to the G)

Have fun playing this – if you're at a party or something, a performance of this piece as written is really a head-turner. Of course, you could always just strum the chords, but you could do that 6 months ago, so why bother with boring play like that now.

Play to your potential. Good luck and good playing.

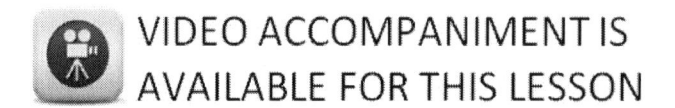

VIDEO ACCOMPANIMENT IS AVAILABLE FOR THIS LESSON

Head to http://learnguitar.nz

The Old Ballad Song

End Verse

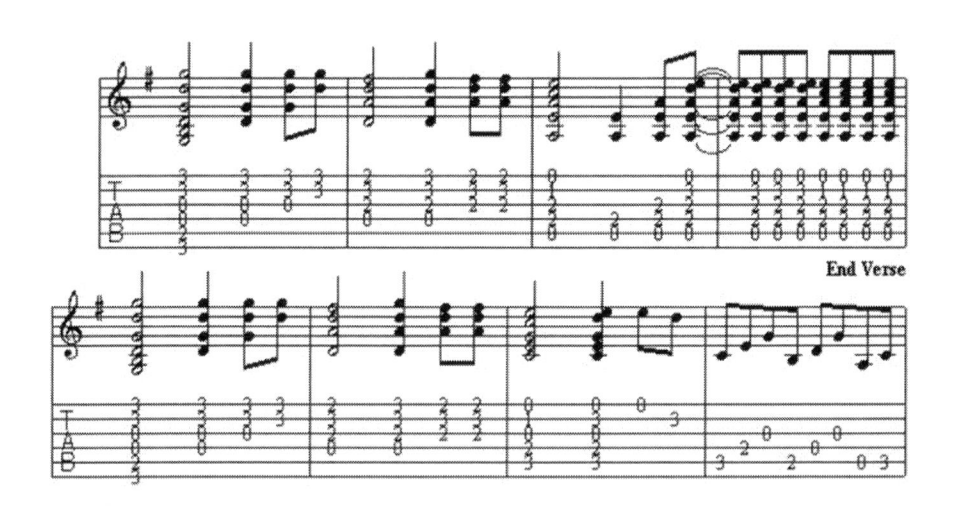

Chorus

End Chorus

2nd Chorus

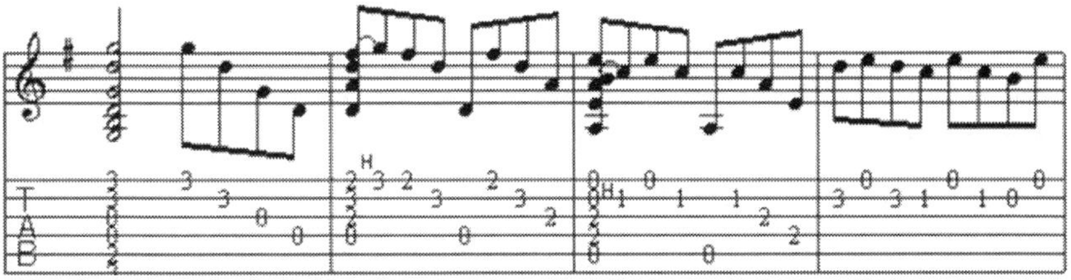

End 2nd Chorus

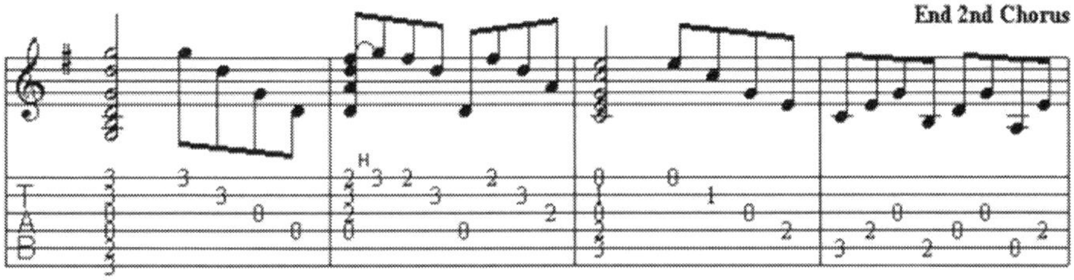

Lead Break

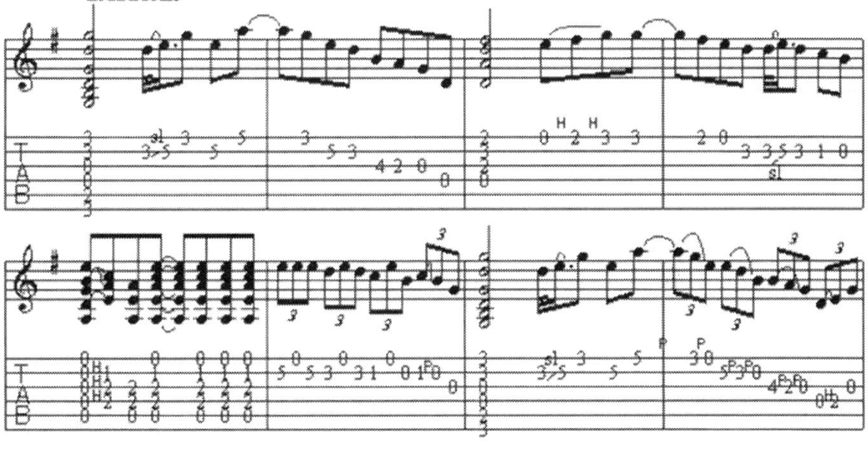

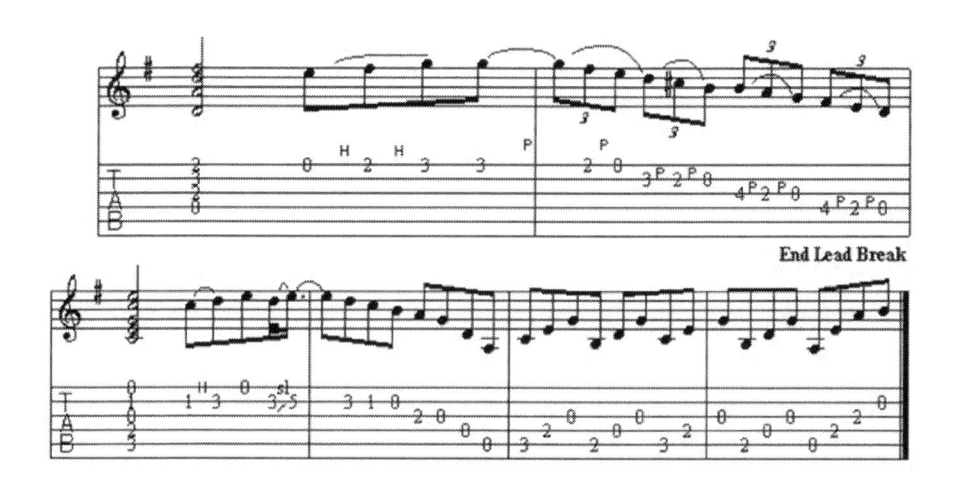

End Lead Break

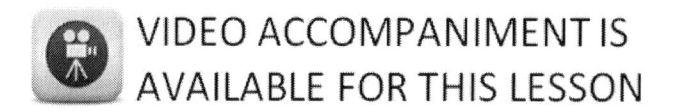

VIDEO ACCOMPANIMENT IS AVAILABLE FOR THIS LESSON

Head to http://learnguitar.nz

HAVE YOU CONSIDERED...

Congratulations on completing *LEARN GUITAR: Intermediate Course.*

If you have enjoyed what you have learned, please consider one of my other titles, available from the website http://learnguitar.nz or from any major online retailer.

Learn Guitar – A Beginner's Course

Learn Guitar fast with this easy-to-follow and unique system. 40 individually crafted lessons teach Open Chords, Barre Chords, Music Reading, Strumming, Theory, Riffs, Scales, Arpeggios, Guitar TAB, Fingerstyle, Licks and more.

Learn Guitar – Advanced Lead Guitar

Electric lead guitar made easy. Practice scales for speed and fluency and learn the entire fretboard for extended soloing. Learn the best techniques including bending, tapping, sweeping, and how to craft an effective lead break for any song.

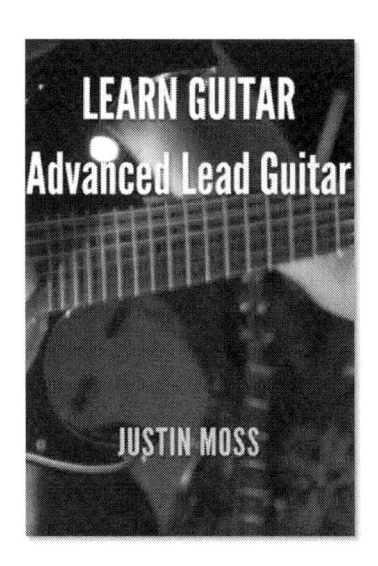

See http://learnguitar.nz for more information.

Printed in Great Britain
by Amazon